## What People Are Saying ...
### *Sharing the Burden* . . .

"When it comes to health care, the choice has never been clearer: Are we going to entrust ourselves to economies of grace, comprised of human-affirming mercy and compassion, or are we going to be overwhelmed by a mass-secularized, administrative state of dehumanizing taxation and regulation? In *Sharing the Burden,* author Michael Miller gives us a vision of what it looks like when we embrace the former. This isn't pie-in-the-sky idealism; this is as real as it gets. From small beginnings to growing pains, from biographies to balance sheets, from bureaucratic battles to the gargantuan threat of socialized medicine, Miller provides for us a memoir of God's providential faithfulness in what is nothing less than a revolution in the ways health care is administered and paid for. You will be blessed by this testimony of the miracles that happen when God's people come together to show the world what a distinctively Christian community of faith, hope, and love can really look like."

**—Dr. Stephen R. Turley, host of TurleyTalks.com
and author of *Health Care Sharing Ministries:
How Christians Are Revolutionizing Health Care***

"This book is an incredible testimony. It's not a testimony about some alternative to insurance products that claim to provide health care. This is about health care the way it was designed by God in the book of Acts. This is a testimony about devoted Christians as members of Samaritan Ministries: a testimony of a body of believers that in the name of Jesus Christ are committed to being obedient disciples for their brothers and sisters. Samaritan Ministries is a living, breathing testimony of the God-given power that is evident when a body of believers becomes willing disciples of Christ. My wife and I are grateful for the opportunity to be a part of this incredible work of faith."

**—Dan Celia, host of *Financial Issues* radio program and founder of Financial Issues**

"This book is a prototype of how a disruptive innovation can develop from the ground up, even when operating out of a repurposed chicken coop. So much of today's "health care" is dictated from the top down, with the top being the supposedly all-powerful federal government. Samaritan, on the other hand, seems to be inspired from the very top, our Creator, and implemented by gifted fishermen, not the academically and politically credentialed elite. The personal stories of those who make the ministry work and of those who benefit from it are featured, along with the nuts and bolts of its functioning and the harrowing tales of the attacks it has miraculously survived."

**—Dr. Jane Orient, executive director of the Association of American Physicians and Surgeons**

# SHARING THE BURDEN

## The Samaritan Ministries Story

## MICHAEL MILLER

FOREWORD BY

### TED A. PITTENGER

Founder, Samaritan Ministries International

**Sharing the Burden**
*The Samaritan Ministries Story*
Samaritan Ministries International © 2019
By Michael Miller with Foreword by Ted A. Pittenger

Scripture quotations are from the ESV® Bible (The Holy Bible, English Standard Version®), copyright 2001 by Crossway, a publishing ministry of Good News Publishers, Wheaton, Illinois. Used by permission. All rights reserved.

Cover Design Credit: Jonathan Herzog

Print ISBN: 978-1-7342106-0-6
eBook ISBN: 978-1-7342106-1-3

For more information, visit SamaritanMinistries.org


Published by Samaritan Ministries International

Printed in the United States of America

Dedicated to the past, present, and future members of
Samaritan Ministries International

Samaritan Ministries International started with a few people in a remodeled chicken coop and has grown to include more than 270,000 individuals among its membership.

Meet the people God used early on to help Christians help other Christians with their health care needs. Read testimonies of God's providence. And learn why believers across the United States and in other countries depend on God's provision through other believers.

# CONTENTS

Foreword  11

Introduction  13

1: Looking in the Mirror  17

2: The Pittengers' Health Care Awakening  25

3: Priorities  39

4: Off the Ground  49

5: Enter Lansberry  69

6: Growing Pains  85

7: It's Not Insurance!  99

8: Mr. Lansberry Goes to Washington  107

9: "A Better Way to Do Things"  129

10: How Health Care Sharing Works  137

11: The Stories  149

12: SMI Is Family  159

13: SMI Is a BIG Family  169

14: Where We Are; Where We're Going  177

Endnotes  189

Appendix 1  193

Appendix 2  195

Glossary  197

Sources                                   201
Acknowledgments                           203
About the Authors                         205
Christians Helping Christians             207

# FOREWORD

It was 2003, and I received a phone call from our local newspaper indicating they would like to do an interview to learn more about Samaritan Ministries. The religion reporter, Mike Miller, came out to our office to conduct the interview. As I recall, the resulting article was pretty good—especially considering that the concept of health care cost-sharing involves a huge paradigm shift and can be difficult to grasp, compared to the more familiar model of medical insurance. Apparently, it was at least good enough that when Mike Miller came knocking again, just a few years later, we were willing to schedule another interview—except this time it was a *job* interview. The newspaper was offering Mike a buyout and he wanted to continue working in the journalism field, but he also was excited about the possibility of being involved in ministry. We were excited to welcome Mike to join us as a Samaritan staff member.

Now, 11 years later, Mike has written a documentary of sorts, telling the story of Samaritan Ministries. And it tells the story of my family's journey in following God's leading. But ultimately, it is a story about Jesus, and the wonderful things He is doing to purify and perfect His bride—the body of Christ.

I was a history major in college, and I was encouraged and excited the first time someone pointed out to me the clever phrasing that history is "His Story." God is weaving a tapestry that involves each of our lives, and what you are holding in your hand (or on your screen) is a faithful record of the story Jesus has written and continues to write.

Sure, it involves the Pittenger family, and it involves Samaritan Ministries—and its members and Board and staff— but, ultimately, everything points back to Jesus, and the story that He is writing. To God be the glory. Great things He has done!

As we celebrate 25 years of ministry, I hope you enjoy reading His Story. God is building His Kingdom, and we get to participate by joining Him in His work. That's why I close nearly all of my correspondence with . . .

For The Kingdom!

Ted A. Pittenger
Founder & President
Samaritan Ministries International

# INTRODUCTION

Samaritan Ministries is an uncommon answer to a common problem: how to pay for medical care.

For most Americans, that has been a problem easily "solved." Get health insurance, right? And, if you can't afford the cost of insurance, get government help.

But is that a Biblical way to take care of your health care needs? Is it good stewardship of the money God has entrusted to you? Is it even affordable, especially for one-income families, single-parent families, and self-employed workers?

Back in the late 1980s and early 1990s, Ted Pittenger decided it wasn't good stewardship. As the owner of a painting and wallpapering business in central Illinois, he believed that Christians could manage their health care needs more efficiently, and from a Biblical foundation. Then, after he and his wife, Shari, became members of a health care sharing ministry, he decided such an outreach could be shaped in better ways. Following the Lord's leading, Ted started Samaritan Ministries International (SMI).

While that is a brief encapsulation of the past, in an era of increasing government regulation of the health care system, the story of SMI also represents the future. As this explanation of Samaritan's origins and operations goes to print, this health care sharing ministry based in Peoria, Illinois, continues to gain thousands of new members each year. Rapidly. There are some earthly explanations for this—as more Christians seek alternatives to Affordable Care Act requirements, they favor free market health care options, refuse to fund abortions, and want to spend less than insurers are charging—but the more likely explanations are divine:

- Health care sharing ministries are a way for the varied members of the Body of Christ to help bear one another's burdens (Galatians 6:2).

- God honors a method of doing things that honors Him (1 Corinthians 10:31).

- God hears prayer (Jeremiah 33:3).

As Ray King, an SMI founding Board member and Special Counsel to the President, says, "Prayer is the foundation of everything Samaritan does. When the ministry faces a turning point, we ask for prayer. When the ministry faces a need, we ask for prayer. When our members have medical needs, we ask for prayer."

Prayer has made Samaritan what it is, from the day Ted Pittenger spent fasting and seeking God's face about starting a health care sharing ministry, to the day political backlash against a health care "reform" bill threatened to require Samaritan members to purchase insurance. Prayer keeps Samaritan members tied together as a sharing family, even if some members come and go over the years.

This is the story of how Samaritan Ministries came into being, how its members have been able to bless each other, how it has become a family inside and outside the Samaritan offices, and how it has survived legislative and regulatory challenges.

# INTRODUCTION

Most of all, it's the story of how God works through His people, the Body of Christ, to help us help each other.

For The Kingdom,
Michael Miller, August 2019

# 1

# LOOKING IN THE MIRROR

When Tracy Kamprath looks in a mirror, she often recalls the time when God blessed her. Granted, in November of 2007, when a doctor diagnosed her with a brain tumor that would leave part of her face paralyzed, it didn't feel like a blessing.

Although she was having trouble with her hearing, she kept putting off going to the doctor. When she finally consulted one, he discovered tumors. Not just the one in her ear; after several scans and follow-up visits, he found a tumor in her brain as well.

An initial visit with a surgeon revealed the estimated cost for surgery for the Chappell Hill, Texas, woman: more than $100,000. In fact, he told her the bills for such an operation commonly reached $250,000. While that wasn't unusual for that kind of surgery, what made Tracy and her husband, Jeffrey, unusual is they had no health insurance—by choice. Instead, they were members of Samaritan Ministries International (SMI), a health care sharing ministry in which members help pay the medical costs of other members.

The Kampraths joined Samaritan in 2004 when both taught at a private Christian school. Unable to afford health insurance, with two teenage boys and a younger daughter, the Kampraths felt exposed, especially with the children involved in sports and the potential for injuries. "We felt like we had to have something," Tracy said. As a result, the couple looked into the three primary health care sharing ministries (HCSMs) at the time—Samaritan, Christian Care Ministry's Medi-Share program, and Christian Healthcare Ministries.

Once the Kampraths learned that Samaritan members share health care expenses by sending money directly to one another, instead of through a central office or a remotely controlled exchange (as the other HCSMs do), they chose SMI. However, even after feeling confident enough to join Samaritan, the Kampraths were still apprehensive.

"Maybe I'm stubborn and have to experience things," Tracy said.

Experience overcame her fears. Before the brain tumor, the family submitted several other medical needs. For example, earlier in the year of her cancer diagnosis, their son, Matthew Aaron, broke his leg. Shares sent by SMI members enabled the Kampraths to pay the bills for his treatment, which totaled about $900. Samaritan "worked beautifully," which convinced Tracy. The Kampraths had some other minor needs met by members—but nothing like the need Tracy learned of that fateful November day. Even with their past positive experiences with Samaritan, the financial prospect unsettled them—especially since Samaritan membership had a limit of $100,000 per need at the time.[1] They would have to find resources for any additional costs.

Tracy panicked, thinking, "What have we done? We don't have insurance!"

Her admission surprised her physician.

"When we first told the doctor we didn't have insurance, he looked at me, dumbfounded, and said, 'You don't have insurance?' He had never dealt with anything like this," Tracy said.

Neither had the Kampraths, but along with their doctor, they were about to see how other Samaritan members would come to the family's aid through financial sharing and fervent prayers. They would get to see Samaritan's signature verse—"Bear one another's burdens, and so fulfill the law of Christ" (Galatians 6:2)—in action. They had a burden; in this case, both financial and medical—and other members of the Body of Christ would share it.

> They had a burden; in this case, both financial and medical—and other members of the Body of Christ would share it.

On that day, though, Tracy sat in the car with Jeffrey after her appointment and cried.

"We can't face this—physically or financially," Tracy told her husband.

Jeffrey comforted her, reminding her of times in their lives and in Scripture when "trusting in God" had looked foolish in the world's eyes, yet things had worked out. It looks foolish to 21st-century Americans when someone doesn't have health insurance—even though that concept is less than a century old—and instead relies on God and the Body of Christ to help him or her bear that burden. The Kampraths were going to trust that people they had never met (and probably never will, at least on this side of Heaven) were going to send them money to help them pay their overwhelming medical bills.

In the world's eyes, the Kampraths' decision to drop health insurance and join a health care sharing ministry was foolish, even irresponsible. But in the eyes of the early Church, it was (and still should be) a natural expectation that we help each other in times of need. After all, the apostle Paul wrote,

"If one member [of the Body of Christ] suffers, all suffer together; if one member is honored, all rejoice together" (1 Corinthians 12:26).

"That was the thing that just kind of thrilled me, to see God taking the thing that the world was saying was foolish and then showing His glory," Tracy said.

God showed His glory through a health care sharing ministry conceived in 1991 by a guy with a degree in classical civilization studies who ran a painting and wallpapering business. Since its inception in October 1994, Samaritan Ministries members have shared millions of dollars in health care needs. The ministry has gone from having only volunteers to hundreds of paid workers. Offices, first located in a converted chicken coop on Founder Ted Pittenger's property, have graduated to these quarters, by turns:

- a garage house

- a former church building

- a former warehouse

- a 57,000-square-foot building with its own warehouse, with a 28,800-square-foot, repurposed roller-skating rink for a second building (purchased later).

As Ted Pittenger and others have followed God's commands to care for one other, hundreds of thousands of people have received help from other Christians in paying nearly $2 billion in medical bills. People like Jay and Lori Moore, who received shares when their son, Collin, was successfully treated for lymphoma in 2007. Or Ron and Debbie Walker, when Debbie was diagnosed with and treated for a brain tumor in 2009. (Debbie went to be with her Lord in 2010.)

# LOOKING IN THE MIRROR

## Samaritan Ministries offers a Biblical way of sharing health care needs that otherwise would represent burdens.

Samaritan Ministries offers a Biblical way of sharing health care needs that otherwise would represent burdens. It's a ministry that allows its members to pay their medical bills without having to resort to health insurance. They rest easy knowing they're not paying premiums that finance abortions or go toward treating illnesses resulting from unbiblical lifestyles. Members send their money directly to other Christians whose Biblical lifestyles have been attested to by their church leaders. They're encouraged in each month's newsletter: "Send a note. Pay your share. Always stay alert in prayer."

Executive Vice President James Lansberry says the model is the church in action. "It's personal. It's community-oriented," he said.

It's a way to practice what Pittenger calls "one anothering" through authentic Biblical community. "I think that's what authentic Biblical community is: caring for one another, praying for one another, bearing one another's burdens, exhorting one another," Lansberry said.

That concept was so essential for Pittenger and others who had input in the early days of Samaritan Ministries that its core documents list it first as one of the ways the ministry carries out its purpose (which is carrying out the Great Commission, found in Matthew 28:18-20):

"Associating within the community of the Christian faith for discipleship, medical-sharing, physical needs-sharing, financial stewardship, evangelical, and educational purposes in accordance with the bylaws of this organization and the laws of the state or states wherein this Corporation may be doing business."

Samaritan has gone from its early years, when new members would sign up only in handfuls, to periods of substantial growth. By early 2018 the numbers reached more than 75,000 member households. The ministry has expanded from its original three employees in 1997 to more than 300 full- and part-time workers, and from tracking members' needs and shares on a 1990s version of Microsoft Access to developing proprietary software and online apps.

SMI has also changed from a "fly-under-the-radar" approach to appearing on the front page of the *New York Times*.[2] As part of the Alliance of Health Care Sharing Ministries, it lobbied successfully for its members' exemption from the individual health insurance mandate in the Affordable Care Act (ACA), signed into law in 2010 by then-President Barack Obama.[3]

But its primary function has remained the same: enabling Christians to help other Christians. Like-minded believers share one another's medical expenses through a unique ministry that doesn't involve insurance.

The concept is simple, but that doesn't make it easy.

## How It Works: The Short Version

The sharing concept may seem complex at first glance, but it is relatively simple, once you get used to sending your shares to other members or receiving shares for your needs. To become a member, you sign a basic statement of faith in Jesus Christ, agree to practice a Biblical lifestyle, and provide verification from your pastor that you do follow that lifestyle and regularly attend worship. You send an agreed-on amount of money each month, depending on the size of your household, directly to another member household that has submitted proof of medical expenses. And, when it's *your* turn, you (like the Kampraths) submit a need-processing form, along with itemized bills from your medical incident. If your need fits the Guidelines and is more than $300, it will be shared among other member households. Those with whom your need has been shared are directed to send their shares to you.

They also are asked to pray for you, just as you have prayed for those with whom you have shared. The Kampraths made that point to their doctor.

"We told him we had thousands of people praying for him," Tracy said.

The answers to those prayers became obvious as 2007 passed into 2008. Tracy walked out of the hospital six days after her operation that spring instead of the predicted six weeks.

"I went home on April Fool's Day, which I thought was God's joke on the doctor," Tracy said.

She cheated the dire predictions that she would have to use a walker or wheelchair, that she would never walk on her own again, and that she would have to use a feeding tube. None of those things came to pass.

And the final cost of the incident, thanks to discount negotiations, ended up at around $55,000, far below the initial $250,000 estimate. The Kampraths received other members' shares, along with cards of encouragement. The discounts were an additional blessing for the Kampraths, who no longer faced the worry of how to pay bills that exceeded the $100,000 limit in force at the time.

"That verse in Ephesians that God will do far more abundantly than all we ask or think . . . that's the verse that kept playing over and over in my head: He's going to do more than we can think of," Tracy said.[4]

He did. In 2009, when Tracy returned to her doctor on April 1—"That's beginning to be my 'good day'"—he told her she didn't need to return for another year. Although she still had a small residual tumor, doctors removed it in May of 2010. Now "[I'm] watching what I eat and put into my body, trying to take precautions," she said.

"It's made me very aware of the gift of life that God's given me and taught me that I need to not go through life blindly," Tracy continued. "I have a little bit of facial paralysis left, but not much. To somebody who's new to meeting me, they can't tell, but to my family, they can see a little bit. To me, the paralysis is a reminder. When I look in the mirror, I think, 'That's okay. That's a reminder of what God did for me.' Not a day goes by that I don't think I'm so fortunate and blessed. It has cemented our belief in Samaritan. There's no doubt in our minds now that it works, and it works beautifully. It's what the Bible tells us to do. We have been passionate about it and very vocal in telling people about it."

The blessings, she said, have flowed as a result of the brain tumor, which enabled Tracy to draw closer to God and to "be able to see Him work through His Body in so many different ways."

"I thank God that we found Samaritan Ministries and that He led us there," Tracy said. "I'm in awe of how He works through y'all and through the Body of Christ and that in this day and age something so simple can have such a profound impact on people's lives."

The path that led to that point, though, was filled with struggles, doubts, and delays.

# 2

# THE PITTENGERS' HEALTH CARE AWAKENING

God began weaving the tapestry that would become Samaritan Ministries International when a young married couple from central Illinois attended a family-training conference in the mid-1980s. Ted and Shari Pittenger were starting their family and looking for guidance in how to build a God-fearing household.

During one of the sessions, a speaker talked about the possibility of starting a health care sharing program similar to one called Christian Brotherhood (now known as Christian Healthcare Ministries), founded in 1982. Brotherhood was modeled after Anabaptist methods of supporting community members with burdensome needs. The speaker encouraged anybody interested to share his or her contact information with him.

Ted and Shari put their names down.

"It was an exciting concept to me," Ted said.

For Ted, "exciting" could explain any concept pointed at furthering the cause of Jesus Christ in the world, especially anything that would deepen one's spiritual walk, as well as the role that families played in the Body of Christ.

## Genesis of a Ministry

Born in 1955 in Mount Morris, Illinois, a small town 100 miles west of Chicago, Ted Pittenger attended church as a youngster but qualified as a "Christian in name only." It wasn't until 1972, during his junior year at Mount Morris High School, that he understood his need to make Jesus Christ his Lord and Savior. This awakening took place during a Bible study at his football coach's house. Ted then got involved in that coach's church and coffeehouse ministry. By the time he headed southeast to the University of Illinois (U of I) at Urbana-Champaign in the fall of 1973, Ted Pittenger stood on a solid foundation of faith.

Initially, he wanted to study architecture at U of I. He had enjoyed drafting class in high school. "I thought, 'Isn't that what an architect does, blueprints and drawings and stuff like that?'" Ted recalled. Besides, he could probably make pretty good money at it, which was important to him. But when he took an introductory architecture course as a freshman, he discovered that not many architects designed houses anymore, instead focusing on "hospitals and schools and larger buildings like that." He had wanted to fulfill his creative bent by designing homes for a living, but now he saw that wasn't likely to happen.

By the next semester, his love of numbers had convinced Ted to change his major to accounting.

"I used to keep track of my own personal finances, and I could tell you to the penny how much I had," he said with a laugh. "That was back when I had 50 bucks. If I bought a five-cent piece of gum out of a gumball machine, I'd write it down."

After he almost failed his first accounting course, though, he decided to veer away from that profession, too.

Then the coach's wife, who had helped lead him to Christ, offered to disciple him, so he decided he would drop out of college for a year for this Biblical training. When autumn came, though, the couple told Ted that the woman wouldn't be able to work with him.

However, he still had direction. Ted headed back to U of I for the spring '75 semester and contacted Jeff Burgard, a student and member of the campus chapter of the Navigators, a nationwide Christian discipling organization. Jeff agreed to disciple Ted.

Ted also settled on a major that semester: classical civilizations. He had set his sights on getting a job with Campus Crusade for Christ (now known as Cru), an evangelism and discipleship ministry he greatly admired. He realized that to get that job he would need a college degree. However, he decided he didn't want to obtain a degree in a high-earning field and then be tempted by a well-paying career that might distract him from ministry.

"I had a fear that I would become materialistic if I became an architect or engineer or something like that, and that materialism would take me over," Ted said. "So I had purposefully gone into classical civilizations, knowing that it was somewhat of a dead end, career-wise. But at least I'd have my college degree so I could go on staff with Campus Crusade."

He ran into a stumbling block when the Campus Crusade ministry in Champaign "kind of fell apart" (although it later bounced back), so he worked with the Navigators. "But I still had this heart for Campus Crusade," Ted said. Once the campus director for the U of I Navigators asked Ted what he'd like to do after graduation. Ted's answer caught him off guard.

"I'd like to go on staff for Campus Crusade," Ted replied.

The director just looked at him, offering a hesitant response along the lines of, "Okay . . . I'm all for that. Not everybody can go on staff with the Navigators, and we'd love to train up some guys and have them go into different ministries."

Ted secured his heart's desire in 1978, when Campus Crusade hired him for its staff at the University of Wisconsin–Eau Claire. He served there three years. In 1979, he achieved another heart's desire—marrying Shari, whom he had met as a fellow student involved with the Navigators at U of I.

But then Ted changed ministry directions, thanks in part to Campus Crusade itself. At a training session, he learned that about 80 percent of American Christians became believers before age 18, meaning that the vital time to reach people is during the first 18 years of their lives. Ted began to feel pulled toward ministry to and through families more than toward ministry with college students.

"I thought maybe families are the more important thing—raising up godly mothers and fathers so they can raise up godly children," he said.

Ted left Campus Crusade in the summer of 1981. Not knowing what else to do for the moment to support their growing family (his first child, Meg, had been born in 1980), the Pittengers moved to East Peoria, Illinois, where Ted soon started working as a painting contractor for a business run by Shari's aunt and uncle. He learned how to wallpaper and paint. The Pittengers' assumption was that Shari's aunt and uncle were going to retire soon and that Ted would take over the business. Soon, though, the aunt and uncle signaled they wouldn't be retiring for some time. So Ted started his own painting and wallpapering business: Pittenger Paint and Paper. In 1982, their second child, Breanna, was born.

All the while, Ted watched for opportunities to return to ministry. In 1985, he even applied to be a painter at Wheaton College, Billy Graham's alma mater, near Chicago. He thought he could start taking classes on the side and get back into ministry that way. Even though he thought the job spelled a perfect match, the college didn't hire him.

"In 20/20 hindsight, that was God's perfect will, but at the time it was really hard on me," Ted said.

By the mid-1980s, after the birth of Jason, their third child, Ted and Shari decided they would homeschool their children. Although uncommon at that time, the practice was attracting an increasing number of Christian families. That focus on the home provided the impetus for Ted and Shari to attend several family conferences, where they first heard about health care sharing ministries.

Until then, the Pittengers had gone without health insurance. They had had some experiences—good and bad—with the health care system. For example, when Jason was 18 months old, he suffered a febrile seizure while Ted and Shari were out of town. Shari's parents, who had been caring for him, took him to the emergency room. Within a few weeks, a doctor prescribed phenobarbital. The barbiturate made the "poor kid like a zombie" for two to three days, Ted said. That was too much for Shari.

"I said, 'No, we're not doing this,'" Ted recalled. "The MD said, 'You're questioning me?' as though he were a minor deity." After consulting with a friend who was a medical resident, the Pittengers were told that the drug was unnecessary, and they started using more natural methods of controlling the seizures.

The condition was ultimately resolved the old-fashioned way: the Pittengers let Jason grow out of it, giving him acetaminophen to head off a fever whenever they sensed one coming on. That sparked a realization that there were different ways of doing things when it came to health care, just as there were different ways of educating their children.

They were given a little off-the-record medical advice after their daughter, Meg—then about three years old—had her elbow pulled out of joint when Dad hefted her up to put her on his shoulders. The Pittengers took her to a local emergency room, where doctors popped the elbow back into joint. Ted's brother-in-law, a physician's assistant, told Ted and Shari that it would most likely happen again, and then showed them how to fix it themselves. Six months later, it did happen again when Ted went to pull Meg up to him while they were watching TV. She cried, but Ted followed his brother-in-law's directions, and the elbow popped back into place.

Shari recalled, "I guess there were a few things here and there that just prompted us to think, 'Oh, you can step out of the mainstream?' There are different ways to do things, even in the medical field. Neither of us had any kind of medical background, but we developed this sense of 'You can question what's going on in the medical field, and you can use your own common sense a little bit, too.'"

Another factor that strongly influenced the early years of Samaritan was input from Gregg Harris's home business seminars. Ted and Shari met with other couples for mutual encouragement and support in both homeschooling and home business. The Pittengers realized that they had a strong desire to be entrepreneurs, to include their children in their work, and to work from home as much as possible.

So, already open to stepping outside the norm, Ted and Shari were interested when they heard about health care sharing.

"I just really liked the concept of helping one another," Ted said. "I liked the idea of the barn-raising mentality."

That concept would stick. A barn-raising illustration—similar to a scene in the movie *Witness,* set in Amish country—of families coming together to help community members in need, provided the inspiration for illustrations in Samaritan's original brochure and early advertising. "It just made a lot of sense," he said. "It was so much cheaper. Historically, that's what insurance was like to begin with. It was a sharing type of ministry."

Mennonites, who share an Anabaptist tradition with the Amish, began pooling resources to help each other out with various financial needs shortly after World War II. Medical costs weren't high enough to warrant health insurance, but the federal government imposed wartime wage freezes aimed at controlling labor costs to support the war effort. That left employers looking for a way to increase compensation and attract good workers, so they did it through health benefits that wouldn't show up as income. The perk stuck, even after the wage freezes were lifted.[5]

Meanwhile, Mennonites and other Anabaptists also had started offering low-interest loans for members of their communities who had debts, like hospital bills. Seeing the need that was out there, the groups began to formalize the procedure; Mennonite Mutual Aid started its hospital aid program in 1949.[6]

"The folks who began Christian Brotherhood had grown up in the Amish and Mennonite region of Ohio, so they just copied what their neighbors did," said attorney Michael Sharman, who has served as general counsel (at different times) for both Christian Brotherhood and Samaritan.

Christian Brotherhood leaders had suggested that any health care sharing ministry startup should have at least 500 families signed up before starting to share needs. Because the earlier effort to start a new HCSM that the Pittengers had signed up for had faltered, Ted and Shari signed their family up with Brotherhood.

"I just thought it was a great idea," Ted said. "I'd share it with friends."

Those friends included DeWayne Arington, a Peoria-area independent carpenter who didn't have health insurance. DeWayne and his growing family—at the time he had three children—attended church with the Pittengers. When Ted told DeWayne about Christian Brotherhood, DeWayne thought it was a unique idea and was interested—until he found out about the alcohol restrictions. To be a member of Christian Brotherhood, you had to pledge to abstain from alcohol. That hadn't been a problem for the Pittengers; Ted didn't partake of the fruit of the vine very often, and Shari never did. But it was a problem for DeWayne, who got together with his dad on Saturday nights for pizza and beer. He didn't want to give up that special time, so the Arington family took a pass on Christian Brotherhood.

Although the alcohol restriction "wasn't that big of a deal" to Ted, he realized that Brotherhood was probably scaring away potential members who liked to have a beer now and then, but without abusing alcohol. In addition, Ted had been thinking that Christian Brotherhood could be marketing differently to get the word out about health care sharing. This valuable idea needed more exposure, he believed. A different approach, using quality materials, improving the guidelines, and allowing modest alcohol consumption (but not to the point of drunkenness), carried significant potential.

While focusing on painting and wallpapering, the possibilities kept gnawing at him. When the monthly newsletter from Christian Brotherhood would arrive, he would crunch some numbers in his head: "X number of ministry members sharing X dollars for X number of needs would require what overhead? How much would be coming into the ministry through fees?" Apparently forgetting his early adjustment of priorities when he discarded the idea of a lucrative architectural career in favor of serving in ministry, Ted started to see dollar signs:

"If there are 20,000 members, and let's say the average member is giving this much, that's a lot of money flowing through this thing. I could probably make some money doing this. This could be a viable business." At the time, a Christian acquaintance named Ray King was helping Ted with painting and wallpapering jobs, so he knew about the struggles to launch Samaritan—as well as Ted's thoughts about the money-making potential of Samaritan. Ray posed a challenging question: "Would you still want Samaritan to succeed if you knew you weren't going to make much money at it?" Ted reflected on that for a while. One day while they were wallpapering, he gave Ray his answer: "As long as God paid the expenses, I would do this for free."

That, Ted believes, was a turning point.

"It was like God kind of sitting up in Heaven smiling, going, 'Okay . . . now you're ready,'" Ted said. "I really had a sense that God wanted me to do this. I still had that kind of nagging sense inside."

Meanwhile, as the Pittenger family grew but their income did not, Shari's parents helped by buying a home for them to renovate and live in. Then, in 1988, when Shari's mother's family farm was up for sale, a relative encouraged Shari's parents to keep the property, which had been in the family since 1837. The Pittengers moved in, renting and making further renovations to the property that would become the site of the first Samaritan Ministries offices.

The Pittengers moved into Shari's mother's family farmhouse, renting and making further renovations to what would become the site of the first Samaritan Ministries offices.

## Legal Maneuvers

About 1991, John Chaney, a friend of Ted and a fellow member of Christian Brotherhood, was looking for work outside of ministry. He had just planted a new church in Peoria, one that would grow to become the largest in the area. However, once he had established Northwoods Community Church, John left that ministry.

"John's an entrepreneur type," Ted thought. "I'll bet he could start a ministry like this."

But when John landed a new job within a few weeks, Ted changed course. He decided to take the business experience he had gained with Pittenger Paint and Paper and start the ministry himself. First, he would have to set up a corporation. To do that, he would have to hire someone from a profession he did not much care for—a lawyer. He contacted a Peoria attorney who identified himself as a Christian. But that lawyer wanted to charge a $1,500 retainer to do research and then advise Ted whether he could proceed legally. Ted did not see the point of that. Christian Brotherhood already did health care sharing. Obviously, it was legal. Ted didn't want to know *if* he could do it. He wanted to know *how* to go about doing it.

So, the painting contractor went to see another Christian attorney. That lawyer, who specialized in family practice, said setting up a nonprofit corporation was outside of his expertise. He referred Ted to Brian Heller, an attorney practicing near Ted's home.

In that July 3, 1991, meeting in Washington, Illinois, Heller didn't quote him an outrageous fee, require money up front, or send him elsewhere. He took Ted seriously.

"Brian has the face of a pretty good poker player," Ted said. "He didn't look at me and say, 'You're an idiot.' He replied, 'Oh, very interesting.' He said, 'You know you need to apply for a not-for-profit status in Illinois, and you need to do this and that.' I said, 'Okay, well, just tell me what to do and we'll do it.'"

Still, back then, the concept of health care sharing was "totally alien" to the lawyer, like it was to 99.99 percent of the American population—Christians included. Heller said that, besides filing incorporation papers, he would have to research Christian Brotherhood's guidelines and see how they had organized that ministry. Heller also advised Ted to create a board of directors with at least three members. Ted did that, turning to local Christian men he knew and respected. In addition to Ted, the other original Board members were John Chaney, Ken Reutter, Eric Ackerman, and Ray King. They were all homeschooling dads. Since then, Ted has often pointed out that Samaritan was founded by homeschoolers with homeschoolers in mind.

Ken Reutter was an accountant who would go on with his wife, Joanne, to be part of the Project Amazon missionary project in Brazil. Eric Ackerman worked for the Illinois Environmental Protection Agency; Ted had led him to Christ at U of I. They would serve briefly in helping Ted get Samaritan started. But the fifth man, Ray King, would become vital in shaping Samaritan.

The son of a Groveland, Illinois, farmer, Ray graduated with a journalism degree from U of I in the spring of 1973 and went to work for the Navigators in Colorado Springs, Colorado, as a writer and photographer. Ray just missed Ted at U of I; the younger Ted arrived on the Urbana-Champaign campus later that year. After working with the Navigators for a while, Ray and his wife, Marsha, moved back to the Peoria area and started raising a family.

God didn't let Ray and Ted miss connecting this time: The King and Pittenger families met through a local homeschooling group in the 1980s. After getting to know each other, Ted and Ray realized they had several things in common: they were both interested in strengthening the Biblical foundations of Christian families, they had both been involved in the Navigators, and they were both self-employed, Ray having joined his dad and brothers in farming.

Ray stopped farming for financial reasons, however, and was "having a terrible time finding work." He painted houses for minimum wage (at that time five dollars an hour) for a month under a man he had met at a Bible study. Then Ted offered Ray a job painting for eight dollars an hour. Ray took it.

As the two worked together on light remodeling and painting jobs, they would talk about men's ministry, homeschooling, family, and what could be done for those ministries on a broader scale. Ted told Ray about Christian Brotherhood, but Ray had his doubts about the lasting power of such a ministry. "It'll work fine for a few years," Ray said, "but there are all kinds of things that can go wrong with it." Ted told Ray that he wanted to start his own health care sharing group by tweaking some of Brotherhood's practices and doing a better job of marketing.

Ray had his doubts about whether such a new, blended business/ministry would succeed. But he also looked at the possibilities from a Biblical perspective.

"One thing I've noticed over the years is that a lot of businesses start up and quickly go out of business—something like a 95 percent failure rate," Ray said years later. "But you cannot always tell what God wants done. Whether it's likely to work is not one of the criteria you necessarily go with. If He wants you to do something, then you need to do it. So rather than saying, 'It can't work,' you say, 'Well, is there anything that we're talking about doing here that is unbiblical?' If we find out that there is nothing in the mix that's unbiblical, then there's a possibility that this is something God wants. So, although I wasn't certain how it'd work, I didn't think it was my place to say it won't work, or you can't do it, or you shouldn't do it."

So, when Ted asked for Ray's help in forming the corporation, Ray obliged, sitting in the Pittengers' dining room and signing incorporation papers with the other original Board members one night in September 1991, giving birth to Samaritan Ministries International.

# 3

# PRIORITIES

The original goal: start sharing needs in the fall of 1992. Ted Pittenger told his children he'd have 100 families signed up by October and then set out to attract interest. To get the ball rolling, Ted, Ray King, and a mutual friend went to the second Promise Keepers conference, held in Boulder, Colorado, in July 1992. University of Colorado football Coach Bill McCartney started PK in 1990, with 72 attendees at its first conference. That number mushroomed to 4,200 at the group's first official event in 1991. The 1992 version attracted 22,000 men, nearly half the capacity of the university's football stadium. While that seemed like a natural place to let heads of households know about Samaritan, only a few men displayed much interest in the concept of health care sharing.

By October, only 10 families had joined, with five more joining in November. Fifteen households fell far short of the 500 that Christian Brotherhood leaders considered the minimum to make a new health care sharing ministry viable.

## What's in a Name?

Meanwhile, Ted and attorney Brian Heller were fighting name wars. Early Samaritan advertising had encouraged anybody interested in being part of the *Samaritan Newsletter* to contact Ted. The name caught the attention of a ministry leader in Indiana, who called the number in the ad.

"The caller asked if this was Good Samaritan Ministries," Ted recalled. "I said, 'No, it's Samaritan Ministries International.' Then this guy just kind of launched this attack. 'This is so-and-so from Good Samaritan Ministries in Indiana, and you guys are causing us a lot of trouble in Illinois because they think that you're us and blah blah blah, and you guys can't use that name,' just really giving me a hard time. I think they may have sent us a 'cease-and-desist' letter. We told them that we weren't going to change the incorporation name, but we would no longer call the publication the *Samaritan Newsletter*. We agreed to change the name for that."

Ted first considered using "Christian Health Care Network" for the newsletter, but he soon discarded that name. Homeschool pioneer Mary Pride told Ted that she thought it brought to mind "network marketing," a concept that might scare away some potential members who'd had bad experiences with multilevel promotions. Ted and Brian also found out around that time that Medi-Share, another new health care sharing ministry, had contracted with a group called Christian Health Care Network for some add-on services.

Finally, since it was a newsletter they were talking about, Ted and Brian settled on *Christian Health Care Newsletter*, a division of Samaritan Ministries International.

The organizers of the fledgling ministry were confused about why other ministries with the word Samaritan in their names were raising such a ruckus. Attorney Brian Heller said the word *Samaritan*, especially used in reference to the story of the Good Samaritan in the Bible, was "kind of like the word *hamburger*," fairly generic.

# A Splash of Cold Water

The name game proved a minor annoyance compared to challenges that the health care sharing concept faced on the state level.

John Hawthorn, a leader at Christian Brotherhood, had called Brian Heller in November 1992 with the news that starting a new health care sharing ministry might not be a good idea at that time. Various state insurance commissioners were starting to give Brotherhood problems, and the ministry had lost a case in the Delaware Supreme Court. Plus, he told Heller, it would probably be more financially sound if Samaritan had 3,000 households to start with, rather than the earlier target of 500.

"That was a bit of cold water," Heller said.

Heller recommended Ted wait at least a year to see how Brotherhood resolved its legal issues.

Ted, operating from the openness and Biblical ethics that would continue to characterize Samaritan's dealings with its members through the years, returned the approximately $1,500 the first Samaritan members had sent to become part of the ministry. He suggested they might want to check out the *Christian Brotherhood Newsletter* because they "weren't going to be able to get this [Samaritan] up and going right now." (Ted and Shari were still Brotherhood members at the time.)

"That was a really challenging time for me because I felt like I was doing what God wanted me to do and it just totally fell on its face," Ted said. "It really prompted a time of searching."

So the Pittengers stayed in survival mode, with Ted running the painting and wallpapering business and Shari helping out where she could with a part-time art and graphic design business while homeschooling the kids.

While they waited, the entire health care industry entered a state of confusion due to an effort to create "universal health care" by Hillary Clinton, whose husband, Bill, won the presidential election in November 1992. Ted's belief that the Lord was leading him to create Samaritan Ministries faltered even more.

## Which Way to Go?

Stuck in neutral by early 1993, Ted wondered whether he should move forward with his idea for a new health care sharing ministry. Pray as he did for weeks on end, he still couldn't get a clear sense of God's leading. As it turned out, the delay proved providential because of a then-budding movement seeking to impose insurance coverage on every US citizen.

Had that effort succeeded, it would have smothered Samaritan Ministries International before the ministry could draw its first breath.

The momentum started with Harris Wofford's surprising victory in a special US Senate election in Pennsylvania in November 1991. Democratic leaders saw the win as a mandate (no matter how slight) to pursue universal health insurance. One of the main movers behind that effort was James Carville, who would go on to manage Bill Clinton's successful presidential campaign the following year. Universal health insurance would then become a prime focus of Clinton's first term, led by his wife, Hillary.[7]

One of the key components of "Hillarycare" (the label that the media and political commentators attached to the Health Security Act of 1993) was an individual mandate requiring individuals to obtain some form of health insurance coverage. Had it become law in the mid-1990s, the noninsurance health care sharing ministries would have lacked the membership and influence that later helped them secure a federal exemption. By 2010, the year Obamacare was signed into law, larger membership rolls and financial resources allowed HCSMs to press for their members' freedom to share their health care needs.

As the health care debate raged in Washington, DC, Ted and Shari Pittenger moved on with life in the "other" Washington (Illinois's much smaller version). Even though the Pittengers were celebrating the birth of their fourth child, Anna, Ted grappled with the direction—if any—of the fledgling Samaritan Ministries. He didn't feel enough people had demonstrated interest to make Samaritan viable. In addition, the legal challenges facing health care sharing ministries nationwide, coupled with the possibility of nationalized health care under a Democratic administration and Congress, produced spiritual confusion.

Ted felt "kind of frustrated with the Lord." He had thought he had sensed God's desire for him and responded by laying the groundwork for a new sharing ministry, but nothing seemed to be working out.

## "Go Forward!"

Ted found an opportunity to seek more clarity when he spent a day alone with God. On July 31, 1993, Promise Keepers held its third outdoor rally, attracting a sellout crowd of 50,000 men. While Ted couldn't afford to go to Boulder, he had heard that a local Christian radio station would air a live broadcast of the event. That would allow him to listen to the messages but also spend time in solitary prayer in a renovated chicken coop on his family's farmstead. Walking into the outbuilding, he flipped on the radio, opened his Bible, and started listening and praying.

Notes in a journal reveal his thoughts from that day:

*I don't want to be in a position of trying to demand something from the Lord, but this situation does make me think of a song by Petra,* I Need to Hear From You.

*Perhaps that is a little arrogant and demanding, but it's the cry of my heart today. "I need to hear from You!"*

*What do I need to hear about?*

*Christian Health Care Network—(formerly known as* Samaritan Newsletter*)—*

*For what it's worth, the first impression I had concerning a word from the Lord is Exodus 14:15:*

*"Then the* LORD *said to Moses, 'Why are you crying out to me? Tell the sons of Israel to go forward!'"*

*And in another place, the waters of the Jordan did not part for the Levites until they put their feet in the waters.*

*Regarding moving forward on CHCN, I've mostly felt quite positive about it. In regard to letting peace be the umpire in your heart (Colossians 3:15), I would say I feel pretty peaceful about it. Any lack of peace comes in regard to money. I just don't know where the money is going to come from. But maybe that's the point—move forward, appeal for funds (and they will come). Plant a little mustard seed, and it will grow. I hope I'm not deceiving myself. I have had some experience with that nagging sense that you are grieving the Spirit. And I don't sense that in this case. Mostly I'm just fearful. Fearful that I'll get myself out on a limb again, and God won't come through. (Even as I wrote that, the impression in my mind was—"Fear not, for I am with you!")*

*I'm fearful that I might be trying to do it in the power of the flesh and thus trying to go against God.*

That day, Ted also journaled his thoughts about whether God was teaching him something through a delay, or the hesitancy he felt over starting Samaritan. Had he placed too much focus on the money he hoped to make? Had he been "deceitful" in his communications by trying to portray the ministry as "already up and going"? Was God sparing him from an early member having a catastrophic need that would break Samaritan's back? Was the Father protecting Samaritan from the type of legal hassles confronting Christian Brotherhood in various states?[8] Had he improperly "presumed on God" and gone into debt in an effort to launch the ministry?

July 31, 1993, proved pivotal for Ted. The next day he recorded in his journal, "I sense a pretty strong conviction to go for it." He talked to Shari about his feeling that "this was something that God really wants me to do," the same thought he shared with Ray King later that week. Ray cautioned Ted about reading too much into his application of Scripture passages, but "otherwise he was generally quite positive and encouraging, something which he hasn't always been and especially so as of late," Ted wrote in his journal. From that point on, as if to confirm God's leading, significant events unfolded.

> From that point on, as if to confirm God's leading, significant events unfolded.

First, Ted received an unsolicited call from Mary Pride, another early leader in the homeschool movement and author of several books. She had heard about his efforts and wanted more information. In addition to her questions about Samaritan, she offered some ideas on how to try to get it moving. Just the fact that Mary had called him out of the blue encouraged him.

After this, Ted called George Sarris, a homeschool leader who gave dramatic presentations of Scripture. He asked George for ideas on how to jumpstart Samaritan from its relative handful of members to 500. Sarris suggested telling people that Samaritan members would be expected to help as much as possible, but to caution they might not receive enough for 100 percent of their medical bills paid each month. Even if a member family received only half its request, it would be better than nothing, Sarris reasoned.

Ted thought the concept—which would come to be called "prorating"—seemed sound. Here's how it would work: when members submitted medical needs that totaled more than available resources for a month, those with approved needs would have them prorated according to the total amount available through members' shares. For instance, if enough shares were available to meet only 80 percent of the total needs, that would be the percentage those with needs would receive that month. While they might not get all they hoped for, they would get something, and the ministry would not collapse from too many bills. Meanwhile, special funds, discounts, and contributions would frequently help to make up shortages.

Eventually, the Samaritan Guidelines would dictate that if shares had to be prorated three months in a row, then the Board would propose a share increase to members for a vote. That way, share amounts could keep pace with the reality of rising health care costs.

With this key decision in place, Samaritan's embryonic development continued. In return for his services as a painter, Ted secured printed materials for the ministry through AccuPrint, a print shop about 30 minutes southwest of Washington. The shop's owners, Mike and Tracy Heine, had met Ted through a Peoria-based bartering group and agreed to his proposal of printing in exchange for painting their house.

Shari worked hard, too, putting her graphic arts talents to use by designing Samaritan's first logo, brochures, other marketing materials, and the ministry's letterhead. Ted also depended on her to proofread materials.

Soon, Ted got back in touch with attorney Brian Heller and said he would like to take another stab at getting the ministry off the ground.

Over the previous several months, the legal climate had improved. Christian Brotherhood attorney Michael Sharman had managed to get seven state legislatures to pass laws saying that health care sharing ministries were exempt from regulation as health insurance entities. That kind of recognition in the law gave them an air of legitimacy.

"We would attack at the regulatory level, we would confront at the legislative level, and we would attack at the judicial level," Sharman said. "Our view was, if we attack enough, we're going to eventually win."

Sharman eventually litigated and won cases in 21 states. This success at the state level—coupled with Hillarycare's fading fortunes and eventual demise in Congress—spelled perfect timing for Samaritan and another health care sharing ministry to emerge.

# 4

# OFF THE GROUND

Just as Ted Pittenger was considering the re-launch of Samaritan Ministries International in August of 1993, another entry into the sharing ministry field appeared.

E. John Reinhold, then the president of the American Evangelistic Association and a former officer with two insurance companies, launched Christian Care Ministry's Medi-Share program that month. Reinhold had been involved with Christian Brotherhood but, like Michael Sharman, had observed some problems with the ministry's transparency, especially on the financial end. Those problems eventually surfaced when the state of Ohio forced the ministry into receivership. (Happily, the ministry later rebounded under new leadership and renamed itself Christian Healthcare Ministries.)

The Medi-Share program differed from Samaritan Ministries' and Christian Brotherhood's approach. Instead of adopting Samaritan's method of members sending shares directly to other members, or Christian Brotherhood's later use of an escrow account, Medi-Share required members to send their shares to the ministry's office. They then paid providers out of a trust. Later Medi-Share instituted "virtual sharing," where members opened accounts with America's Christian Credit Union and had money transferred between accounts.

The ministry also emphasized disease prevention—including a vegetarian lifestyle—and good health, including offering members health coaches' consulting services.

Medi-Share saw rapid growth its first year, attracting 1,000 households (and reaching more than 150,000 by 2019). This was probably owing to the American Evangelistic Association's strong reputation in the Christian community since the 1950s. However, it also used a stop-loss insurance policy for large needs. That practice would eventually cause the ministry trouble in Kentucky, where the state Supreme Court would rule in September 2010 that Medi-Share was a form of insurance and subject to regulation as such. By that time, though, Medi-Share had dispensed with the policy. It finally resolved matters with the state of Kentucky, partially due to the state legislature passing a clarification of its "safe-harbor" statute in 2013. That legislation verified that sharing ministries could operate in Kentucky without fear of violating insurance law.

It took Ted until the fall of 1994 to get Samaritan Ministries underway. Initially, that didn't amount to much. Ted had told his kids—again—that Samaritan would get 100 members the first month. They fell far short. Only 10 households—including the Pittenger family—signed up in October 1994 (considered the ministry's birthday). At first, shares were based on "units," with one unit (one person) priced at $40 per month, two units (two people) costing $80 a month, and a share of $120 per month for three units, which included a family of any size. Those households that chose the moderate-alcohol-use option paid higher amounts: $50, $100, and $150, respectively.

Among those early members were James Reid and Paul and Elizabeth Garcia:

**James Reid of California.** A self-employed freelance cinematographer and operator of a Steadicam—an invention that stabilized handheld cameras to allow for more flexible filming in the field—James felt pressure to find some kind of health care provision for his young family. However, $600 to $700 per month (pretty steep in the 1990s) for health insurance was too much. "That was a house payment," he said. "It was out of the question." After praying, he discovered a startup called Samaritan Ministries via SMI's ad in the classified section of *WORLD* magazine. He signed up as the ninth member in history and is still part of the ministry.

"Their overall plan of attack was much more Biblical than 'Send your money to an organization and they'll manage it,'" James said.

**Paul and Elizabeth Garcia of Georgia.** The Garcias enlisted as member household number 10. As sole proprietor of his dental practice, Paul struggled to find affordable health insurance. Even after he secured a policy, outside of group rates their premiums would "go through the roof" each time they had a baby, Elizabeth said.

"Just because we used it," she said. "We got tired of that."

After hearing about Samaritan from friends, they decided to give it a try. They especially liked the ministry's willingness to share maternity needs and desire to keep membership amounts low. Like James Reid, they are still with the ministry more than 20 years later.

"It has remained affordable, and it just worked," Elizabeth said. "We haven't had any problems with it."

Back in 1994 and '95, growth came sporadically, with a monthly average of about five new members. Still, it steadily increased, thanks to the ministry's direct mail literature and paying to have postcards inserted in advertising card decks. Meanwhile, even if Dad's predictions hadn't quite panned out, the kids eagerly helped by stuffing, licking, and stamping envelopes—even 1 1/2-year-old Anna.

# SHARING THE BURDEN

Ted decided that he could more easily focus on launching Samaritan if he had some free time during the day, so he divested his business operations to give himself fewer responsibilities as the owner. He went to work for Caterpillar Inc., the heavy equipment manufacturer, during a strike by the United Auto Workers that had started in June 1994. "I liked to make the distinction that I wasn't a scab," Ted said. "A scab is a union guy who crosses the picket line. I wasn't a union member, so that would make me a strikebreaker."

The second-shift factory job posed its challenges, though. "Ted had to drive an hour to the company's Pontiac, Illinois, plant to work on a machine that performed the final metal lathe work for fuel injectors." Suffering from the effects of an odd schedule, Ted occasionally experienced problems staying awake after working a full shift—plus occasional overtime—while driving back home through monotonous farm country. "I'm sure I drove off the road at least twice," Ted said. To decrease the likelihood of an accident, he carpooled sometimes and occasionally stayed overnight at the home of Ray King's brother, Tim, in Pontiac, waking up at 8:00 a.m. to head home. While at home, Ted could work on Samaritan matters before heading back to Pontiac for work in the afternoon. Even with a one-hour commute, his more regular schedule also allowed him to spend more time with his family, which continued to grow, with Bethany being born in the spring of 1995.

One time, Ted had some Samaritan work that "just couldn't wait," so he took his computer with him. The next morning, instead of going home after a few hours of sleep, he stayed at Tim's home to enter addresses into a database for four hours. He neglected, however, to save his work. When the time came for him to leave for his shift, he turned off the computer . . . and four hours of work fizzled into nothingness.

Despite this lapse in recorded history, Samaritan Ministries proceeded to make its mark by slowly gaining traction. The ministry passed its first real financial test in June 1995. Until then, SMI hadn't faced any substantial bills—just a few hundred dollars here and a thousand dollars there. Members (or newsletter subscribers, as they were called then) saw their needs met in full each month.

Then a member who had a hysterectomy submitted expenses of $10,000. Ted gulped when he surveyed the available monthly shares: about $2,500.

Prorating got its first workout.

Ted wrote a letter to the woman to let her know how much in shares she could expect to receive the first month, and that "we'll see what happens next month." After four months, the need had been met in full. This was possible only because "God hadn't given us very many other needs" at that time, so Samaritan members concentrated their shares on paying her bills.

"That was kind of a big faith test," Ted said.

Although SMI passed that test, growth continued at a halting pace. By September 1995, shortly before Ted was laid off from Caterpillar, Samaritan encompassed only 55 households. Shari remembered doing the math, and it didn't look good: at that rate, it would take Samaritan a decade to surpass the 500-member "minimum" level. "But that's okay," she thought. "We'll just keep plugging along."

Meanwhile, someone who would believe in Ted's efforts was trying to get ahold of him.

## Help From an Unexpected Source

During the fall of 1995, attorney Brian Heller called Ted to tell him that Michael Sharman—who had served as general counsel for Christian Brotherhood—wanted to talk to him. Sharman had helped Brotherhood survive some regulatory and legislative challenges, as well as get legislation passed that allowed health care sharing ministries to operate without being regulated as insurance. Assuming Sharman wanted to talk him out of developing Samaritan any further, he didn't bother calling him back. When Sharman didn't hear from Ted, he contacted Brian again. Brian called Ted again and told him that Sharman "really" wants you to call him and advised him to return the call because he believed Sharman wanted to help.

When Ted finally called, he was glad he did.

"Christian Brotherhood and I have had a parting of the ways," Sharman told Ted. Still, the attorney had a passionate belief in the principle of medical needs sharing. "I've looked around the nation at what's going on, and I like what you guys are doing, and I'd like to know how I could help you," Sharman said.

"We don't have any money," Ted confessed. "There's no way I could hire you to come help me."

"We can work that out," Sharman said. "I like what you're doing. I like the model. I'd be willing to work for free for a time to help you get going."

But Sharman's offer had a catch—the right kind. He would help Ted only if the Samaritan Founder wanted to be legal *and* Biblical. That's what Ted wanted, too, which resolved that matter. After all, Sharman pointed out, if a health care sharing ministry does things in a spiritually proper manner, "then you do wind up in that very narrow region of legality." Otherwise, it ceases to be a ministry and ends up being insurance.

"There isn't a lot of flexibility in insurance laws for congregated health sharing that should not be regulated as insurance," Sharman said later, speaking from his practice in Culpeper, Virginia. "The way Samaritan does it comes into that very narrow area. The reason it's a very narrow area is that one of the main definitions of insurance is that it's a risk and a promise to pay for the risk. So if the entity gives either an implied or express promise to pay for the risk of the health problem, it's insurance. It doesn't matter what you call it, it's insurance. And the cases and regulations and statutes say that. So that's why it's important to have it clear that there's no guarantee. People need to know that very clearly."

A health care sharing ministry (HCSM) also has to make it clear that it does not require actuarial studies to determine premium rates. If they do these things, health care sharing ministries run the risk of being regulated as insurance, which would take away their freedom to operate by Biblical guidelines. Membership requirements, such as signing off on certain statements of faith and pledging to live a Biblical lifestyle, likely would be disallowed. An HCSM wouldn't be able to decide which needs would be acceptable to share and which wouldn't be (such as abortion). Plus, they would be required, like insurance companies, to compile large reserves. Samaritan had been specifically designed, through member-to-member sharing and prorating, to avoid that.

"We don't need those kinds of reserves, because we aren't holding the money," Ray King said. "Our members control their money. Our members do the giving directly to each other."

In his conversation with Ted, Sharman asked the $64,000 question: How many families did Ted have signed up?

"Sixty-five," Ted said.

That wasn't exactly what Sharman expected to hear.

"I wish I could have seen his face," Ted said. "I think he choked. He said, 'Sixty-five?'"

Still, Sharman continued, "I can work with that."

Ted was delighted. "Landing Michael Sharman as Samaritan's attorney was like a semi-pro basketball team getting

Steph Curry to play for them—for free," Ted said. Sharman had already helped, telling Brian earlier that year Samaritan needed to change its ads; the text sounded dangerously close to an insurance pitch.

"Don't do anything that gives them an excuse," Sharman advised—meaning an excuse to regulate.

Even when he worked with Christian Brotherhood, Sharman supported the development of other health care sharing ministries so Christians who wanted to opt out of health insurance or reliance on government had more than one option. That need became even more emphatic after the Democratic Party's bent toward universal health insurance surfaced. So even while working with Brotherhood, Sharman didn't mind advising Brian during SMI's setup phase. He was more concerned that a ministry have "both economic and spiritual integrity."

"What one health care sharing ministry does well helps the others, and what one does badly hurts the others," Sharman said.

Because of the same concerns that prompted John Reinhold to start Medi-Share, Sharman cut ties with Brotherhood and offered to help Ted. After informally advising SMI for two years, he signed on as general counsel, working solely for member donations. For the first years, he saw his main duty as saying no.

"No, you can't change this. No, you can't change that. No, you don't want to say this. No, you don't want to say that."

His goal: to keep Samaritan as close as possible to the post-World War II Mennonite Mutual Aid format. That approach can be best stated as "We're just a bunch of churches getting together to share one another's needs."

Meanwhile, membership numbers continued to inch upward. In June 1996, Ted tried to encourage his family in their efforts by making what he thought was the safest bet yet: If Samaritan had 1,000 members by the same time the next year, he would buy them an above-ground swimming pool to reward them for their help. All five kids, now ages 1 to 16, helped by stuffing envelopes, licking stamps, and collating materials. At the time, Samaritan had about 180 members, and it had taken 22 months to get those. So, gaining more than 800 new households within a year represented a long shot at best.

Then the floodgates opened, and the Pittenger children began looking forward to swimming in the result. Ted made plans to keep his promise.

"I don't know what happened," Ted said, "but by June of '97, we had a thousand members, and I had to buy a swimming pool."

One of the things that had happened was a share increase for Christian Brotherhood members in the fall of 1996 that made Samaritan's share levels more attractive. In addition, Sharman had sent an advisory to Brotherhood members who had been financially supporting him. He let them know he was now working with Samaritan Ministries. As a result, nearly 100 people, many of them former Brotherhood members, joined Samaritan in December alone. A month later, another 100 joined.

## Early Help

Suddenly, in God's timing, hard work and prayer came to fruition. As a result, Samaritan needed to hire some employees. That, however, wasn't a problem. Steve McHugh, a friend of Ted's from the church they both attended, had started painting for Ted. Initially, Ted had asked Anthony Hopp, a college friend of Steve's, if he wanted the work, but Anthony was involved in a Christian singing group and couldn't fit Samaritan in around the group's schedule. So Ted hired Steve, who helped with painting, cleaning out Ted's barn, and various construction jobs.

Although Ted had carefully explained Samaritan's approach, Steve still didn't get it.

"I thought it was weird," Steve said. "I was still steeped in non-Christian worldviews. I thought, 'It doesn't seem like it'd be very secure, the idea of people all over the country sending money to you. How much can you trust that?' It takes a while for it to sink in."

Steve's reaction mirrored that of many when they first heard about Samaritan Ministries: doubt, mistrust, skepticism, or confusion.

Even though he didn't quite grasp the Samaritan concept, Steve trusted Ted enough to say yes when Ted asked if he would like to do some data entry for the ministry. Having done that for IBM as a temporary office worker, Steve was used to typing. And although he was a music major at Eastern Illinois University (EIU), he had some basic experience with computers.

Steve started working half days entering data for Samaritan and the rest of the day painting, wallpapering, or whatever else Ted's business needed done. In the fall of 1996, the two of them worked in a 180-square-foot office in the renovated chicken coop, several feet from the Pittengers' back door. The ministry's only computer was perched on a desk, surrounded by stacks of magazines. Steve remembers having to "weave your way through" the piles to reach the desk.

"I think he got annoyed with me always sitting at his desk, so he finally got a second computer," Steve said.

A family from nearby Pekin—Frank and Kari Lewis and their sons, Jonathan and Matthew—also offered to help. The Lewises had met the Pittengers at a cookout for homeschooling families in the summer of 1995. When Ted told the Lewises about Samaritan, Frank said they didn't know what to think. However, the family liked the idea, because Ted wanted it to be a family-centered effort, and that was the Lewises' "heart-beat." Already knee-deep in the homeschooling movement, the couple would go on to create and publish the magazine *Home School Enrichment*. Before that happened, they got knee-deep in Samaritan Ministries when Ted asked for help with mailing and database work. They agreed to volunteer, figuring it would teach their teenage sons some business skills.

Later, the Lewises would become contract workers for Samaritan, then full-time employees. They put together Guidelines booklets, initially folding and collating the pieces by hand before turning to a folding machine that lightened their load considerably. They also tabulated demographic information received from surveys distributed through card decks, with Ted hoping to build special-interest mailing lists to sell as a supplement to Samaritan's income.

The Lewises became a source of printed materials. Using equipment they had leased for another project, they printed SMI's subscription forms, Guidelines booklets, and prayer guides. They also handled potential member inquiries, special mailings, and bulk mailings, and prayed over most materials before they went into the mail. At first, they did everything by hand in the 800-square-foot apartment where they lived prior to moving to their current home in 1998. Until 2003, all printed Samaritan materials went through their home. Perhaps most importantly for operations, the Lewises also collated Samaritan's monthly newsletter. The family picked up the materials at Samaritan and usually had them back to the office less than 24 hours later. Staffers would then stuff share slips into the envelopes along with the newsletter and mail the packets to members.

The Lewis family finally had to stop working for Samaritan because *Home School Enrichment* (which they started in 2002) took so much of their time. By the end, between Samaritan and *HSE*, the four Lewises were working the equivalent of three full-time jobs.

The family also offered input on Ted's early vision of how to market Samaritan. The Founder would frequently visit the Lewises for late-night brainstorming sessions, sometimes staying at their apartment as late as 2:00 a.m. to discuss ideas.

Early marketing took the form of setting up booths and speaking at homeschooling conferences and placing ads in card decks sent out to mailing lists. The decks consisted of small advertising cards offering free information or samples of products to a targeted audience. Early on, that audience originated with the burgeoning homeschool movement. Ted figured homeschool families were already doing something out of the ordinary, so health care sharing instead of insurance wouldn't mean a huge paradigm shift for them. Samaritan also started placing display ads in homeschool magazines and conservative venues like *WORLD* magazine. They even advertised in Shari's newly created coloring book for family devotions called *Listen, Color & Learn*, in which she created illustrations for all 150 Psalms.

One of the earliest forms of Samaritan marketing, which continues to be its strongest, was rewarding members who recruited new members.

One of the earliest forms of Samaritan marketing, which continues to be its strongest, was rewarding members who recruited new members. Adapting an idea from Christian Brotherhood, Samaritan started giving a credit toward the monthly share to anybody who referred a new member

Reflecting early years' shares, at first the credit was $40. By 2014, it had risen to $180, before eventually settling in at the current $100.

As marketing produced results, it also demanded changes in Samaritan's operations—such as paying people.

## More Space, More Employees, and Paychecks

In 1996, Ted still wasn't drawing a paycheck; Steve McHugh worked as an independent contractor. After the surge in memberships in late 1996 and early '97, that had to change. Thanks to his foresight, Ted had started saving $100 for each new member. When membership reached 300 by the end of 1996, that meant savings of $30,000. At its next meeting, the Board decided Samaritan could afford to pay Steve, Ted, and Ray King, who became the ministry's first employees in February 1997.

After six years of working on (and for) Samaritan without compensation, Ted would finally draw a salary for his efforts.

Meanwhile, employees had new office space waiting for them. Ray and his son, Kevin, had rewired the Pittengers' small garage house, located several feet south of the chicken coop. The building went up as a garage during World War II to circumvent rationing restrictions on construction materials and then morphed into living space for Shari's aunt and uncle, who helped run the family farm. Now referred to as "the little house," it served as Samaritan's new headquarters.

Ray's main responsibility was using his journalism background to edit the monthly newsletter sent out with members' share assignments. Ray shaped the newsletter to make it a vehicle for expression of a Christian worldview—not just in health care, but all of life.

Like most original employees at Samaritan, Ray ended up doing a bit of everything else, such as answering phones, processing needs, entering data, or putting together mailings. For filing and secretarial work, SMI hired a woman most members in recent years have come to know well (at least by sight). As of this writing, Tina Morris appears in a picture with her husband, Jason, at the top of each monthly paper share assignment sent to Samaritan members—and also in several early promotional photos. Tina and Jason knew Ted from church; Jason grew up on the same street as Steve McHugh. Before long, Jason would be working at Samaritan as well.

Before Jason came aboard, though, Ted sought the man he had first asked to help him out: Anthony Hopp. Anthony had been a music major with Steve McHugh and Jason Morris at EIU. A native of Aurora, Illinois, Anthony had moved to the Peoria area in 1994 to be part of the a cappella singing group For Heaven's Sake. Still working as a substitute teacher in the public schools, Anthony often received calls at 5:00 a.m. telling him where to report that day. The irregularity was growing old.

Like many people in those early days, Anthony didn't understand the concept of health care sharing at first. Although he knew Ted to be a man of integrity, Samaritan still sounded like "pie-in-the-sky good intentions," not a rational way to meet health care expenses.

When Anthony arrived at Samaritan, he set out to relieve the ministry's paperwork nightmares. Stacks of inquiries and applications were waiting to be entered into the database. At first, it was hard for him to gain traction. Not only did he not grasp how the ministry worked, he typed via the "hunt and peck" method. However, as he plowed through data entry and then helped with other aspects, he caught the vision. Ironically, Anthony later helped impart that vision to people interested in joining. As the Membership Development Director, he would oversee staff who answered the phones and explained what the ministry is and how it works. He also weighed in on marketing decisions.

Jason Morris arrived soon after Anthony did. At first a part-timer, Jason juggled SMI with his For Heaven's Sake duties. Jason was already familiar with Samaritan—somewhat. Steve McHugh would tell him about "this crazy business that Ted was starting up on the side that was all about health care and paying medical bills."

"When he explained it to me, I would kind of glaze over, like, 'Sure, whatever,'" Jason said.

Doing music ministry didn't pay the bills for Jason and Tina, though, so they were "busy, busy, busy." Jason waited tables and did some substitute teaching while pursuing a music career. He needed a more flexible work situation that would not interfere so much with his concert schedule. Steve McHugh told him that there might be some work for him at Samaritan.

This time, his eyes didn't glaze over, although he recalled, "I have no idea why Ted actually hired me. I told him, 'Look, man, the group is my priority. I'm supposed to be out singing. I see this music ministry as a long-term thing in my life. What I need is totally flexible work hours, but I can give you what you need when I'm here.'"

"Okay," said Ted, never a man of many words.

Starting at nine dollars an hour, Jason would go into the office as late as 1:00 a.m. to process checklists—forms on which members receiving shares would check off who had sent them assigned shares. Work would pile up in Jason's absence, but he assumed he would be at Samaritan only until For Heaven's Sake caught on. Actually, for some time Ted had contemplated forming a partnership between Samaritan and a musical group so the musicians could promote Samaritan during their tours, a tactic Christian Brotherhood used. Although Ted got the members of the musical group to work for him, the promotional bit never panned out. Eventually, music became a sidelight for the singers, who put more focus on the growing Samaritan Ministries.

In those early days, Jason did anything related to Member Services or Operations, helping Steve out wherever needed. "Steve McHugh was the brain of that thing," Jason said. "Steve was kind of the operational center."

Thanks to Jason, McHugh also received the nickname "Hey, Steve." Sitting at a desk in the small house's kitchen/dining room, "every 30 seconds" Jason would turn to look at McHugh in the dining room as he posed a question—always prefaced by "Hey, Steve." Years later, Morris would get his own nickname, "The Forehead of Samaritan Ministries," based on the camera angle of the photo that went out with share slips.

Ray and Ted also worked in the 800-square-foot garage house—Ray out of the house's bedroom (next to the bathroom, where promotional cassette tapes were stored in the bathtub). With parking for only three or four cars on a graveled drive between the little house and the Pittengers' home, most employees and visitors had to park near a utility shed 100 yards away and hoof it over to the building.

After surveying the sparse conditions, a business consultant suggested they add some ambience to the surroundings. He noted that mud splattered onto the garage house's front window by a vehicle had simply been left to dry. That inspired Shari Pittenger to become the unofficial "Director of Ambience" as she again put her graphic design talents to use. She decorated the little house and later the ministry's other buildings (including the current 57,000-square-foot and 28,800-square-foot facilities).

Soon, the ministry had to expand back into the chicken coop, allowing Jason Morris to impress callers by telling them he would have to transfer their call to the ministry's "other building." SMI remodeled the rest of the coop, thanks in part to the arrival of carpenter DeWayne Arington, who had taken a pass on health care sharing plans several years earlier because of Christian Brotherhood's non-alcohol requirement. Since Samaritan permitted "moderate" alcohol consumption, DeWayne signed his family up in July 1997. An independent carpenter since graduating from high school in 1978, Arington had never done desk work. But when Ray King called DeWayne several months after he joined to ask if he might be interested in working for Samaritan, DeWayne seriously considered it.

"I was at a point where I was tired of what I was doing, so I desired to do something different . . . but I'd never done anything different," DeWayne said. "I was more used to being told, 'Here are some tools—go build this,' and that's what I did. To take away the tools and shove me behind a desk just seemed wrong in some ways, or just outside my realm of experience. The biggest part probably was coming to the point where I was comfortable believing the Lord did have something different for me to do, and this might be it."

He thought about the offer for a while, prayed about it, and decided he could make the transition. However, there wasn't much desk work waiting for him at Samaritan. At least, not right away. So, he set out to frame, drywall, and wire the rest of the chicken coop, allowing Ray and Anthony to move their desks into that building. There was a problem, though: it had no windows—at least not on the wall in front of Anthony. That threw Hopp off balance; he asked for a window. Ray found one on the cheap: it had a scratch on the frame. DeWayne cut a space through the concrete block and drywall that he had just finished hanging, and Anthony had his window.

"DeWayne would never let Tony live that down," Jason said.

Eventually, the remodeling and maintenance work slowed, and DeWayne learned more about the ministry by opening and processing mail. As he became familiar with the Samaritan Guidelines for sharing needs, he started working with members. He would later oversee all these duties at Samaritan when he served a stint as head of both Member Services and Operations. At the time, though, Member Services consisted of only DeWayne and the new kid in the camp, Dwayne Carr, another EIU music graduate.

DeWayne grew into his new job, especially as he warmed to the ministry's mission.

"It was a fun time. I enjoyed it," he said. "I didn't know I could do something different, but once I started doing this, I really liked the opportunities I had to minister to people. I can do the paperwork, and that's okay. I can make phone calls and take care of different business, and that's okay. But I really enjoy the opportunities I get to pray with members and encourage them in their walk. I think that's why, as I look at the departments in Samaritan Ministries, I say, 'You can't get any better than Member Services, because that's where you get to do that kind of stuff.' That's the most exciting part of what we do, at least for me—that personal interaction with the members and helping them right at that point of need at that point in time."

He also grew in his ability to work with people with a different personality or approach to dealing with people. Ray King, for instance, is easygoing and flexible in many ways. Arington describes himself as "more rigid."

"I had to learn a lot of that flexibility, to be willing to work with the spirit of what a guideline is saying while trying not to break the Guidelines and working with them to meet needs," DeWayne said. "I guess Ray and Ted trusted me with having principles to make proper decisions."

Making proper decisions at a higher level was the responsibility of the Board of Directors, and it was time to start electing its members. Attorney Sharman had strongly suggested that Samaritan have three Board members elected by the overall membership to maintain proper ethical transparency. He encouraged another attorney, Bill Kurth, of Iowa, to run for the first opening. Originally a member of Christian Brotherhood, Bill helped represent it—along with Sharman—when Iowa's insurance regulators tried to regulate it. Brotherhood went on to win the case at the Supreme Court of Iowa in 1998, but by then, Sharman had left the ministry, and Bill had also departed from the case. Bill and his wife, Karen, joined Samaritan in April of 1996 as the 124th member household.

At Sharman's prompting, Bill ran for the Samaritan Board in late 1996 and has been a member of that group ever since.

"I saw what was going on in Christian Brotherhood, and I tried to warn them of the difficulties they were going to have," Bill said, explaining why he wanted to be on Samaritan's Board. "I wanted to make sure Samaritan never had those kinds of difficulties."

The next Board member elected wouldn't serve very long at all in that capacity. Instead, James Lansberry would usher in the next phase of Samaritan's development.

# 5

# ENTER LANSBERRY

James Lansberry is many things Ted Pittenger is not: Tall. Imposing. Dark-haired. Extroverted. Talkative. Sonorous.

Still, he and Ted share some key passions: for Christ, for family, and for health care freedom.

In 1998, the Pennsylvania native gave his three months' notice to the McDonald's franchise owner he worked for in South Carolina. James wanted to move on but wasn't sure to where or to what. He and his wife, Theresa, had joined Samaritan in May of 1996 (member household 130) and were looking at the possibility of starting a Chick-fil-A franchise, returning to school, or pursuing other options.

James immediately latched on to the Samaritan concept: freedom from the strictures of health insurance, freedom to help other Christians, and freedom to build up the Kingdom of God—all at the same time. When the next Board seat came open for election in 1998, he decided to run, and automatically assumed the position when no one filed to run against him.

When Lansberry traveled to Washington, Illinois, for his first Samaritan Board meeting, he enjoyed "some good discussions with Ted and Ray." So good, in fact—and so impressive—that a few weeks after James returned home, Ted and Ray called

Lansberry to offer him a job as Director of Operations. After accepting, James started in February 1999.

Moving his wife and three children a third of the way across the country hadn't been at the top of Lansberry's list of things to do after leaving the McDonald's franchise. However, his passion for Samaritan's approach to health care got the better of him.

"I really believe in what we do here, so the thought of having it be my vocation, to be involved in it, and to be able to collect a paycheck for doing what I love, and being a part of something I firmly believe in, was just exciting for me," James said years later. "I was able to come up and use my gifts for the good of a ministry that I believe in."

Two decades later, James still believes in it, serving as the ministry's Executive Vice President, its most avid "evangelist" of freedom for health care sharing, and the Founder of SMI's maternity-care charity, called the Morning Center. However, when James arrived in 1999, his primary responsibility involved improving Samaritan's need-processing operations. While not necessarily disorganized, the ministry needed a more stream-lined and efficient way of handling paperwork.

"I think if any of the members had seen what we were doing, they would have jumped ship," Jason Morris said. "It looked so 'mom and pop.'"

No automated processing existed (*that* would take several more years). A Windows-based database contained the mem-bership list. When it came time to send out share slips, Ted wanted as informal a look as possible, so he nixed windowed business envelopes—at least, for a while. Originally, everything was coordinated by hand instead of the computer allocation program now in effect. Terry Kruzan, the programmer who would later help develop the allocation engine, encouraged this handwork, because it would help define the process needed for the computer program. Also offering insights were software developers Mike Monahan and Don Bowen, both friends of Ted.

Share assignments would be printed out several to a sheet on standard-sized sheets of paper and then cut into slips. Informing subscribers how much money to send and to whom, these slips were inserted into newsletter materials. After employees affixed mailing labels and stamps, newsletters went into the mail. However, as the number of members grew, this process proved unwieldy. Leaders recognized the need for a new method, albeit one that still contained a hands-on feel.

Other parts of the process received only minimal computer assistance. For example, one of Jason Morris's jobs involved creating a monthly spreadsheet for listing members who were sending checks in one column and designated recipients in another. He would then copy and paste groupings of names into a word processor to create checklists for members receiving shares. Those households would inform the Samaritan office whether they had received all assigned checks and, if not, who had failed to send them. In cases of a missing check, Jason would highlight the name of that family and mail them a reminder.

At that time, Jason seldom had the option to email members, because in the mid-1990s the internet was still more a curiosity than a fact of life: "I was doing everything by phone and snail mail."

In addition to enhancing need processing, Lansberry also managed people, provided infrastructure, and resolved member complaints. Although initially reviewing the ministry's books to make sure he had a good grasp of financial operations, he eventually handed that responsibility to others. Until the need for someone to coordinate public policy arose, James spent his days mostly "trying to train up a management team and encourage them and teach them to do a little more problem-solving in their areas."

Along with his efforts to increase Samaritan's efficiency, James and others made sure to retain a "personal touch" as much as possible. They strove to ensure that members, prospective members, and others who called Samaritan still heard a human voice on the other end of the phone line.

"I never like it when I call a credit card company and it takes three pushes of the buttons to come close to speaking to a live person—if you can get one even then," James said. "I like to be able to talk to someone. I think many people are like that. We want to make sure we're available to pray with our members when they need us and not look at them as an account number. Numbers can be helpful when you get up to 13,000 households, but we do all that internally. We try to make sure as we're dealing with them to call them by name, asking them how they prefer to be addressed."

Samaritan was able to maintain this policy until membership grew beyond 30,000 households. In order to more effectively serve members, the ministry finally had to install an automated answering system, but one that is still designed to get callers to human beings as quickly as possible.

Despite the progress Lansberry and other leaders achieved, serenity didn't always prevail. Because sinful human beings made up the headquarters staff, conflicts could—and did—occur. Jason Morris and James Lansberry, in particular, did not hit it off.

"When James showed up, I wanted to kill the guy," Jason said. "He butted heads with a lot of people. I dreaded going into work because James had his thumb on me like I was a kid working at McDonald's. Which is another thing, like, 'Ted, what did you do? You hired a guy from *McDonald's*?'"

The irritation went both ways.

"I know I drove him completely berserk," Jason said about James. "Instead of having a godly response to this thing and just confronting him in love, I was exercising rebellion and a real horrible attitude to him as my leader, and I regret that. It was just rude, but I had not learned how to deal with conflict in a way that was Biblical. He'd pull me aside and say, 'If I'm causing difficulty for you, you need to tell me clearly.' And I would confront him with things and, to my great surprise, he would receive it and make changes. I had never met somebody who would just receive criticism or confrontation. James Lansberry has taught me more about conflict resolution and being direct and confrontational in a way that's calm and loving than anybody else in my life."

Jason also credits James with being one of the primary reasons Samaritan still exists—and indeed thrives—today.

"He's got a mind to understand the big picture at all times and to be decisive and direct and not just let himself get run over," Jason said.

Other conflicts involving James Lansberry would arise, mainly over theological issues, but they were always handled by leadership in Biblical ways that not only usually led to reconciliation but also cemented the unity of the ministry.

## Flying the Coop

In those early days, the ministry felt precarious at best. One day 13 new memberships might arrive in the mail, followed by two the next day, and none the day after that. Jason Morris said he and other staffers would joke about the odds that Samaritan would still be around a year later.

"We felt close to the edge a lot," Jason said.

Still, with membership steadily expanding, SMI needed more employees, which brought a corresponding need for more office space. By 1999, it became obvious two small buildings weren't enough for a dozen employees. Wanting to add space without incurring debt—still a guiding policy today—leaders sought an existing building to avoid the prohibitive cost of a new one. SMI's low annual fee had prevented the ministry from setting aside much of a reserve for a building. So, in February 1999, the ministry asked members to consider donating to a building fund.

Reflecting their continuing faithfulness, members donated $50,000 by the end of the year.

"Several friends with experience in fundraising campaigns have expressed amazement at the dedication and generosity of you subscribers who have given to this fund in spite of the fact that you haven't had a definite plan to focus on," Ted wrote in his January 2000 "State of the Newsletter."

Now equipped financially, leaders first considered a former gas station and auto parts store. When that didn't work out, they looked at an old radio station building less than a mile from Ted's property. Ted, James, Ray, and the others came up with a unique proposal, one that would keep the ministry out of debt. However, it caught the sellers off guard. The offer: Samaritan would pay half the cost of the building as a down payment and pay the other half over the next two years. If the ministry didn't come through with the remainder, the sellers could take back the building—and keep the down payment.

"They kind of freaked out," Ted recalled. "'What? You might give it back to us?' It was a total disconnect."

While their approach didn't work with that building, it succeeded with another. Ted heard about a church building for sale in Marquette Heights, a few miles southwest of Washington.

When ministry representatives took a look at the former English Lutheran Church building, the owners asked for $180,000. Ted thought it could work, assuming they'd be able to get enough donations from members. Still shunning debt, Samaritan offered $100,000 as a down payment, with the balance of $80,000 to be paid within two years. Again, if the ministry failed to raise the full purchase amount in that time, the money paid to that point would be considered rent, and the building would revert to the current owners. However, the two parties also agreed that if Samaritan could pay off the balance in one year, that would lower the purchase price by $10,000.

The church's leaders agreed quickly, with the deal coming together in days instead of weeks.

"We realized that all this waiting [for a new building] was because God had this all worked out, and we had our members praying for us," Ray King said.

When raising funds, it also helped to be frank with members about the ministry's needs, Ray said.

"We've always had an attitude where we try to be honest with our members and tell them where things are at," he said. "There will probably come times when it will be important that they know we can be trusted, and so we're not going to try to fool them. We're going to be honest, just tell them what the situation is, and let them respond appropriately."

A surge of new members also meant an influx of sign-up fees, which contributed to the money needed for renovations to Samaritan's new headquarters. Quickly, the ministry flew the coop and closed up the office in the little buildings where everything began.

Still, changes at the new office took several months to complete. The ministry replaced the heating, ventilating, and air-conditioning systems, installed new carpeting, and put up drywall to create offices and a conference room. Workers had to run wiring to network computers together (the wiring hub still hangs from the wall in an old office). By June, the new offices were ready.

After years of being able to take just a few steps to reach Samaritan's headquarters, Ted Pittenger had to drive to work. Meanwhile, Shari found herself adjusting to her husband's noon-hour absences, which felt strange after his eating lunch with the family daily for several years. She also had to get used to the idea that the ministry, which she had helped Ted bring into reality, had grown beyond a close-knit family initiative and into a combination ministry/business. She did not feel part of the communication loop anymore. Before the relocation, Shari knew all staff members and their families and even hosted some early staff events in their home. The staff would also miss out on home-made cookies and interesting visits from the young Pittenger kids. But the move did not end the family-friendly atmosphere that was and still is an important element for the ministry.

> But the move did not end the family-friendly atmosphere that was and still is an important element for the ministry.

Despite those personal adjustments, Samaritan marked a new wave of growth. The early 2000 move tripled Samaritan's office space. The new quarters included a conference room, fashioned just above the former sanctuary, with a large window overlooking the Member Services area. Former Sunday school rooms and the nursery morphed into offices. Desks and cubicles lined the walls in a U shape on the south side of the room and created pathways to offices on the north side. In the kitchen, Ted hung cabinets, while Steve McHugh put down ceramic tile flooring.

The reverberating acoustics at the Marquette Heights building made for some interesting working conditions. The wooden, vaulted ceiling caused practically any conversation to echo around the central room, and sometimes around the offices as well. Even Ted, ensconced in an office down a hallway and near the doorway to the parking lot, could hear what transpired in Member Services.

And there was a lot going on.

## Samaritan's "Next Nine"

By the end of 2001, Ted and Shari's last child, Ben, had been born, and Ted's vision was obviously bearing fruit. Samaritan membership had mushroomed to 7,000 households, surging by 1,000 in 2001 alone (much of it due to problems at Christian Brotherhood). That meant the average monthly total of shared needs surpassed $900,000.

Overall membership growth stemmed primarily from the world's oldest marketing tool: word-of-mouth advertising. Certainly, card decks, magazine articles, radio spots, websites, and conference booths played a role, but personal recommendations have proven the best form of spreading the word. Currently, between 60 and 70 percent of new memberships start with nonmembers talking to members about health care choices, according to Samaritan Marketing Director James McDonald VI. In many cases, pastors ended up joining after signing so many congregational members' renewal forms they decided to investigate this health care alternative for themselves.

More members, of course, meant more work, which necessitated another round of hiring. If the men who had gotten

Samaritan moving in the chicken coop and little house were the ministry's equivalent of NASA's pioneer astronauts nicknamed the Mercury 7, then Bryan Evans, Micah Repke, and others were its Next Nine. More members and staff also meant more information to be handled, which required developing new procedures and policies. That included the creation of departments to streamline operations. Anthony Hopp became a one-man Subscription Development department (later known as Membership Development). That involved taking calls from people wanting to know more about the ministry and sending out informational packets when requested. With interest in Samaritan growing at a rapid clip, that spelled a lot of long hours and busy weekends.

Jason Morris found himself running Member Services along with DeWayne Arington. With his calm, thoughtful demeanor, DeWayne had assumed the role of handling difficult calls—especially those regarding needs that fell outside the Guidelines—and Special Prayer Needs. He shared the management load with Morris, kept busy dealing with individual problems in Member Services, answering questions, and training specialists as they came aboard. Finally, Lansberry decided that since Morris and Arington were "playing" co-managers, they should be recognized as dual department heads over Member Services.

"That was an interesting time," Morris said. "DeWayne and I got along very well. We're very different. We complemented each other."

Jason described himself as "very decisive," but said DeWayne "would be a guy who wanted to kind of analyze for a while before he decided."

"It would drive me a bit crazy," Morris said. But, he added, he probably drove Arington crazy sometimes, too: "My decisiveness would be wrong sometimes, and we'd find that out after the fact. If we had taken time like DeWayne wanted to, we wouldn't have made those mistakes. But we also made some progress because we didn't analyze everything to death."

Other new employees came aboard:

- Cameron Easley, who became familiar with the ministry by delivering Schwan's frozen foods to Samaritan employees and would end up later managing Member Services.

- Dwayne Carr, by then a member of For Heaven's Sake, who worked originally in Member Services and then in Membership Development.

- Rob Stewart, who wanted to quit his retail job so badly that he accepted a position at Samaritan for $7.50 an hour, just to prove he wanted to work there, eventually becoming Operations Manager and later overseeing Mail Operations.

- Seth Ben-Ezra, an old friend of James Lansberry, who started in Member Services and would later migrate to Information Technology Services.

- Micah Repke, a wet-behind-the-ears kid who became a Member Services fixture.

- Bryan Evans, who came to Samaritan from the restaurant industry. He would end up as Samaritan's Vice President for Member Services (before leaving to serve as a pastor) and become one of Ted's designated Board members for a while.

Bryan had spent most of his working career at Monical's Pizza, a chain operating primarily in Illinois and Indiana. He started waiting tables at the Pekin location a few miles southeast of Peoria, then moved to the Champaign, Illinois, outlet.

Eventually, he opened a Monical's in Decatur, Illinois, before moving on to a larger store while developing a reputation as a good "store opener."

After a brief stay in an Amish-type community in northeast Missouri, Bryan and his growing family landed back in Pekin. Bryan got a job at a gun shop. In order to take care of his family's health care needs, the Evanses joined Samaritan Ministries in February 2000.

Samaritan appealed to Bryan—always the Christian libertarian—not just because of the community aspect but also because of the noninsurance model. What eventually also appealed to him was the prospect of a job at SMI. He heard about the opening through Jonathan and Matthew Lewis, whose family was still handling most of the mailings and printing. Bryan contacted Samaritan and interviewed with Lansberry for a job. The interview included a mild confrontation—Bryan brashly told James that James was too liberal. James hired him anyway (later telling Bryan he appreciated his honesty). Bryan started in Operations in July 2000 by updating a database created from responses to an old card deck advertisement before moving into Member Services.

One of his early experiences as a Samaritan member cemented his bond with the ministry. A couple of weeks after Bryan started work at Samaritan, Kim gave birth to their fifth child, Levi. Granted a week's paternity leave, Lansberry assured Bryan he could make up the time as he was able, which Bryan did by working Saturdays. During Kim's recovery, Samaritan staffers he had known only about a month showed up with food for the family.

Then Levi fell ill from *E. coli*, and the outpouring of care continued. After all the gifts of food, the response overwhelmed the Evans family and confirmed to Bryan that he was in the right place.

Kim's maternity need was published as a Special Prayer Need of more than $20,000. It didn't qualify as a regular need, because she was already pregnant when the Evanses joined Samaritan. In addition, costs arising from complications during the birth couldn't be shared. The Evanses' church had contributed some money to help but then advised Bryan to go to the state of Illinois for the rest. The family chose not to do that. Instead, Bryan said, the Evanses got to "see the Body of Christ function" as their mailman brought "stacks" of letters every day stuffed with checks and notes. They ultimately received more than $7,500 in gifts from Samaritan members.

"That was my introduction to Samaritan Ministries," Bryan said. "I'd had a vague idea of how it worked but going through that process was a real eye-opener."

After working in Member Services for a couple of years, he moved into Membership Development, sharing an office with Anthony Hopp. He called the experience "complete insanity." Their office at the Marquette Heights building was dubbed the "clubhouse," a place where people came to hang out during their break, because music and laughter often filled the air.

One of those who hung out there wasn't even an employee—at least not at first. A driver for Schwan's, Cameron Easley followed a route that included Samaritan's Marquette Heights building. He routinely chatted with Jason Morris, Dwayne Carr, and Anthony Hopp during deliveries, turning into a clubhouse regular. He finally asked Jason whether he should submit his resume. Samaritan leaders didn't pursue the lanky Easley, however, thinking he made a much better living as a deliveryman and wouldn't be interested in working there. Once they found out otherwise, they quickly hired him.

"To this day, I'm known as the Schwan's man" in the Samaritan offices, Cameron said.

Also arriving in 2000: Micah Repke, a 21-year-old "kid" who would become a fixture in Member Services. Micah had spent more than five years in Brazil, where his parents were missionaries, before his father moved the family to Peoria after accepting a pastorate there. Ray King had offered a job to Micah's father, Rodney, but Rodney didn't need it. Micah, however, needed at least part-time work while attending a junior college to prepare for a career as a firefighter.

When Micah arrived, he joined Dwayne Carr and DeWayne Arington in Member Services, where he would put out other types of fires for years to come.

"The very first phone call I took was from a woman who was expecting," Micah said. "I had asked her about sending an itemized bill. She got very angry with me. On a later call, she seemed very nice. I've learned a lot about Member Services and being on the phone since then"—like how to calm down upset people.

"Sometimes it's better to listen and not speak, or to talk more slowly," Micah said.

A major personnel change happened in 2001: Michael Sharman, who had been the ministry's general counsel since 1995 after leaving Brotherhood, stepped down. Replacing him was Brian Heller, who had been the ministry's local counsel from the start. Heller had attended most board meetings and helped with accounting and property matters. He remains Samaritan's general counsel to this day.

Heller's love of dealing in regulations suits him well for helping formulate and update SMI's Guidelines, which define the extent to which needs can be shared. Samaritan requires nearly two-thirds of his time. The rest of his legal practice is devoted to setting up corporations and handling wills, income tax work, and real estate matters. Heller says he and Samaritan are a good fit. He knows the needs of the organization and communicates well with the leadership team, which he described as "great." Attorneys with larger practices "couldn't be in any way as plugged in" as he is with Samaritan's everyday workings, he said.

He wasn't totally plugged in right away, though.

"I was their lawyer and was skeptical for years," he said, admitting lingering doubts about the viability and dependability of health care sharing.

So skeptical, in fact, that he didn't join Samaritan Ministries until 1999, after he had to fight with his health insurer over covering his wife's C-section. Even then, he bought his family a high-deductible health insurance policy, still worried about the "big need" that might exceed the ministry's then-$100,000 cap.

Samaritan, however, was about to address that concern.

# 6

# GROWING PAINS

The skyrocketing cost of health care is a primary driver behind the growth in health sharing plans. Even with discounts, expenses can run into the tens of thousands—or even hundreds of thousands—of dollars. In its early days, Samaritan could meet members' needs in a timely fashion by operating with a per-need limit of $100,000 and its pro rata system. Amid spiraling health care costs, the lack of the latter safeguard caused struggles at the Christian Brotherhood ministry that had originally inspired Ted Pittenger to form SMI.

Indeed, problems at the Ohio organization had caught the attention of state authorities. With members' needs piling up, Brotherhood's lack of organizational transparency and accountability compounded those difficulties. In addition to the state stepping in, coverage from a television news magazine boded ill for Brotherhood—and sharing plans in general.

Members started leaving Brotherhood, with many opting to join Samaritan. Rather than rejoicing over a "competitor's" problems, in its newsletter Samaritan called for prayer for the troubled ministry. A front-page story in the November 1999 issue acknowledged that some of the increase in SMI subscriptions had stemmed from problems at "another needs-sharing ministry."

Early in 2001, the state of Ohio placed Christian Brotherhood in receivership—a type of bankruptcy in which a court-appointed custodian oversees an organization's assets. A month later, Samaritan again asked for prayer. The primary request was for God to provide for Brotherhood's members, many of whom had medical bills piling up in the system. Unlike Brotherhood, Samaritan shared what it could each month and postponed additional needs to the next month. If it looked like even that would cause further delays in sharing, needs would be prorated. However, with no prorating system in place at Brotherhood, needs were outstripping available shares. Members who were left waiting for money to arrive still faced medical providers demanding payment.

To reassure its members, Samaritan's newsletter pointed out the differences between the two ministries' sharing approaches. Telling members that they wouldn't face the same kind of scenario as Brotherhood's members, SMI again urged prayer for them.

"Please pray for God to intervene in a miraculous way in the problems the other ministry is having," it read. "Pray that the believers involved would deal with the situation in a Biblical way and not resort to the world's methods of handling problems. . . . Pray that the entire Body of Christ (that includes us) would be alert to find ways to minister to these other members of the Body who are hurting."

Happily, Brotherhood made necessary changes, including naming a new president and CEO. After its release from receivership, the ministry reorganized as Christian Healthcare Ministries. With its troubles in the past, CHM saw increases in membership and today remains one of the two largest health care sharing ministries, with more than 180,000 member households.[9]

## The Birth of Save to Share

While Samaritan's pro rata system kept needs from overloading the ministry, SMI leaders understood that health care economic realities meant members had to deal with "the big picture," which had been a concern among the Board directors for many months.

"What about a $1 million need?" asked many potential—and current—members. "What if someone develops cancer that requires extended treatment? What happens in the event of a heart transplant?"

Although rare, the possibility of such needs arising lingered in the back of people's minds. Early in Samaritan's history, it set the $100,000 per-incident limit because too much over that amount could rapidly sink the ministry. For a while, Samaritan—proudly a noninsurance health care alternative—found itself in the awkward position of pointing out that people who worried about catastrophic needs could buy a high deductible health insurance policy that would kick in at $100,000 and cover any needs above Samaritan's cap.

"We weren't recommending it. We were just letting them know," said Bryan Evans.

At the time, Samaritan leaders knew of only one insurance company offering such a plan: Mutual of Omaha. One day that company contacted SMI to say it had dropped that plan. That's when Samaritan's leaders knew the time had come to offer a plan for bills that exceeded the $100,000 limit.

SMI launched Save to Share in 2002 as the ministry's answer to the million-dollar-need question. Based on a similar Christian Brotherhood program, any need higher than $100,000 (a cap raised to $250,000 in 2010) would be shared by members who opted to join Save to Share. But the leadership struggled with the logistics of handling that large a sum. Initially, the approach involved taking the amount over $100,000 for a need, dividing it among the number of members in Save to Share, and having each Save to Share member send an additional check to the member with the need that month. After 3,000 members signed up for Save to Share, however, leadership realized that meant anyone with the significant need would have the administrative burden of processing 3,000 checks on top of dealing with their health burden. In addition, any Save to Share need would have to be at least $3,000 over $100,000. With amounts less than that, it would end up costing almost as much to mail the check as its face amount.

Eventually, the Board adjusted the program so that members of Save to Share sent out only one check—their regular share plus their Save to Share amount. Thanks to computerization, SMI worked out a plan that accounted for Save to Share amounts and balanced them with overall shares and needs.

A few years later, SMI created another "add-on" program known as Samaritan MV (Motor Vehicles). Until then, few needs resulting from motor vehicle accidents were shared due to Guidelines restrictions. Besides, most auto insurance policies offered high hospitalization coverage. But prospective members were concerned about related needs, because treatment for injuries from serious accidents could sometimes pile up during a patient's recovery. When some states started lowering the amount of hospitalization coverage auto insurance companies could or were required to offer, it made the need for a solution for Samaritan members obvious.

After several SMV development meetings, an advisory ballot went out to members, who indicated they would like to see an additional ministry created to handle such needs. Despite some wrestling with amounts and procedure, SMI implemented

SMV in 2006. During its existence, the plan cost members only an average of two to three dollars per month.

Several years later, though, leadership recognized that the small percentage of SMV needs being submitted—compared to the cost of administering the program—made it impractical. In 2011, Samaritan merged the sharing of these needs into the basic sharing ministry and amended the Guidelines to include needs arising from motor vehicle accidents.

## Birth of a Groundhog

The implementation of Save to Share in 2002 came amid a five-year growth spurt that started in 1999. God's providence was evident as the ministry moved into its larger Marquette Heights facility just in time. The membership increase produced new revenue and more people willing to donate to a building fund. The result: Samaritan paid off the balance of the new headquarters' purchase price in one year, saving $10,000. Building fund donations also paid for renovations and new office furniture. In what seemed like a wisp of time, SMI went from operating in cramped, shared offices with one bathroom and no lunch area into a building with separate bathrooms for men and women, a conference room, larger offices, and individual employee cubicles.

Despite this growth spurt, in Seth Ben-Ezra's eyes, Samaritan was still in its infancy when he arrived in mid-2002.

Seth grew up in an Erie, Pennsylvania, pastor's home frequented by a young man named James Lansberry. "My family made a habit of taking people under their wing, and he was one of the first ones we did that with," Seth recalled.

James and Seth attended the same small college in South Carolina. After graduation, Seth moved back to Erie, while

James married Theresa and started working for McDonald's. After Lansberry arrived at Samaritan, he encouraged Seth to apply for a job with the ministry, too. Seth resisted until he started having job problems. A position at Samaritan opened up in December 2001. Until then, Seth had been a law librarian and closed-file clerk at a law firm in Erie. Then he tried to get an associate degree in computer science after having "kicked around with computers as a kid," including teaching himself about databases.

When Seth arrived at Samaritan in June 2002, he started in Member Services, then named Subscriber Services.

"The 'SS' jokes were fairly thick," he remembered. "Subscriber Services was an insane place to work. There was always a sense of some crushing deadline bearing down on you. I know that's the case now, but it was even more so then."

However, this insanity inspired Seth, stirring up his gift for determining ways to make systems work better. Upon his arrival, Ben-Ezra immediately set to thinking about how he could refine and enhance the Samaritan subscriber database program. In the meantime, he savored the thrill of working on the "front lines."

"You have the opportunity to be talking to hurting people, which means you have the opportunity to minister to someone," Seth said. "By and large, working in Member Services means you have a bunch of people calling you and they have problems. You're trying to be patient and work through that. I actually have a lot of respect for the guys who plug into that and do that well."

In addition to ministering to hurting people, such specialists must be able to turn on a dime emotionally, going from a sensitive situation to paperwork to database work to a member ecstatic over healing and then back to paperwork.

When Seth looks at Samaritan Ministries, he sees a foundational structure with Member Services as the "house," and other departments playing a supportive role to strengthen the structure. Member Services sits at the pinnacle and other departments all play a supportive role. His time in MS gave him a sense of that department's workload and wide range of tasks specialists have to juggle: creating needs for members, tracking bills for those needs, updating files for changes in a member's family and life, and creating and passing along prayer requests.

All of these tasks intensified as membership grew. When Seth arrived, Samaritan was using Microsoft Access to manage its database. Several things about it proved awkward, such as that a Member Services specialist could open only one member record, and one need record, at a time. Specialists could move back and forth between the two types of records but had no way to set something aside on a computer when the phone rang and then return to that spot. So, when a specialist was in the middle of working on one record and received a call from a different member, he would have to close the current record to open the record of the caller—while keeping track of what he was doing before the second member called. It grew more complex when a third member called while the specialist updated the second member's record before he could return to the first member's record.

"There was a sense of, 'What was I doing again . . . ?'" Seth remembered.

As more families joined Samaritan, prompting further development of the ministry's Guidelines, that meant continually updating the database with additional options so new information could be recorded and tracked. "Add a button" became the catchphrase for adding options (and still is).

As a result, "there were buttons all over the place" in the database program, Seth said, "at the bottom of the screen and running down the side. There was an awareness that this was getting to be not a good thing."

Yet leaders also recognized the need for Samaritan to create the solution to its problem.

"You can't go and buy Health Care Sharing Ministries Version 4.0 off the shelf," Lansberry said. "You have to look at what you're doing and then figure out a way to write software that will do what you need."

Seth's desire to make need processing and accurate record-keeping easier for Member Services specialists, while still being able to connect with a subscriber on a personal and spiritual level, provided him with special motivation. From it sprang the foundation of what would be called—inelegantly but affectionately—Groundhog.

One feature desired in a new system was to allow all bills related to a specific need to be entered under one need key. Previously, if members sent groups of bills for one need at different times—say, one on October 1, another on October 15, and another on December 1—the staff had to generate three need keys, with the first being a primary need key. The other two keys would somehow point back to the primary one. But that also meant that specialists would have to track (by hand) how close a need came to the $100,000 per-need limit. Then there was the challenge of factoring in reductions to accurately reflect the publishable amount once all bills were submitted.

It was a kludge (pronounced "klooj")—software that was "clumsily designed or improvised from mismatched parts,"[10] Seth said.

So, he sat down on a Friday afternoon and figured out a way to relate all bills to a specific need while allowing specialists to work on multiple records at once. He sketched out a diagram with four numbers that had to work together—"Now it's more like 14 numbers," he said—and ran it by the guys in Member Services. They poked at it, trying to find ways that it might fail, while Seth explained why it wouldn't.

"It was holding up," he said.

At the time, Steve McHugh was working with computer programmer Terry Kruzan, who worked for the Veterans Administration in St. Louis. Terry had relatives in the Peoria-Pekin area with connections to Samaritan. One had mentioned that the ministry was looking to revamp its system, so Terry visited Samaritan in the late 1990s, while the ministry was still at the Pittengers' property. He offered to help them "on the side." Initially, Terry improved SMI's version of Access and helped the staff maintain the program.

When it came time to start updating the database program again, Seth tossed out his ideas at a preliminary meeting—which led to a "big meeting" in November 2002. Kruzan visited again, and Seth, Steve, and others spent most of the day trying to attack the system Seth had proposed. Once again, it held up. The conclusion was that a new application, designed from scratch and specifically for Samaritan, needed to be (and could be) written.

At the end of the meeting, Steve McHugh turned to Seth Ben-Ezra and said, "Welcome to IT."

As work on the new program began, the ministry made procedural changes to accommodate it. For example, bills were first entered by Operations before handing them to a Member Services specialist. The idea was to get need processing to match the new software by the time it went live so the shift would be less jarring. "Which was good," Ben-Ezra said, "because it was a fairly jarring shift." Programmers Kruzan and Ben-Ezra developed the program after getting wish lists from Member Services advocates on things like forms, capabilities, and workflow.

Meetings typically convened three mornings a week in the upstairs conference room overlooking Member Services. Jason Morris, Seth Ben-Ezra, Micah Repke of Member Services, and—occasionally—others, like Bryan Evans, attended the sessions.

"I'll bet we were nine months doing that, figuring out the next question and the next detail," Morris said. "It was painful."

James Lansberry wanted the program to be released by February 2004, but Seth and Terry, who had started work on it in January, both told him that there was "no way" they could meet that deadline. They told him it would probably come out several weeks later.

"Even writing it in two to three months was pretty astounding," Terry said.

One thing the program's creators lacked, though, was a name.

"I had been shopping around for a name, but nothing good was coming up," Seth said. "*Groundhog* ended up floating out because James wanted it out by February. So it would be done in February or it would see its shadow, in which case, it would come out later. And that's what happened."

According to Seth, Terry wanted to name it SMI Support Center, since software usually has a goofy name in development stages but a more formal one when released.

"The response was, 'We're Samaritan Ministries. We like goofy names,'" Seth said.

While the official name of the program is Samaritan Ministries Support Center, to everyone who uses it, it remains Groundhog. At one time, when a user opened the program, a cartoon or photoshopped picture of a groundhog would pop up in various guises, depending on the season or the chief programmer's whim. That means the little critter has appeared basking in the sun as well as driving a race car. His (or her; the gender is not clear) face still graces the program's icon.

Although consistently updated over the years, Groundhog will eventually give way to a new database—nickname unknown at this point—that will meet the needs of Samaritan's growing membership and take advantage of increased computational capabilities.

## On the Move Again

Within four years of moving to Marquette Heights, SMI faced another space shortage. Back at the Pittenger property, the ministry had squeezed 14 employees into less than 1,400 square feet at one point. Now, 36 employees worked in 4,500 square feet. Leadership asked members to pray again when membership topped 10,000 households. The growth made the need for a larger building more obvious. While initially entertaining the idea of expansion, zoning problems deflated that possibility. So, ministry officers began looking at different buildings. While several building owners extended some offers, the deals either fell apart or the facilities were "snatched out from under us," Ray King said. Some would have taken a lot of work to be made suitable. Others were way too big. Like Goldilocks, Samaritan kept looking for a building that would be just right.

> Like Goldilocks, Samaritan kept looking for a building that would be just right.

The search led to a former combination office/warehouse in Peoria on Altorfer Drive. Situated on the west side of the

Illinois River, a telemarketing company had most recently used the building. But SMI directors weren't sure they wanted it, since they preferred to avoid city congestion. Besides, the $1.2 million asking price was double their $600,000 budget for a new building. Still, the real estate agent handling the Peoria property suggested Samaritan make an offer. So they did—at half the asking price. The owners countered with $900,000. Figuring to sell the Marquette Heights building for $250,000, ministry directors negotiated a final price of $850,000, contingent on the sale of their current building. With computer cables, phone lines, and cubicles already in place, the space offered a lower remodeling cost. So, the ministry made a $50,000 down payment on the building.

However, to maintain sufficient operating funds to keep the ministry going until it finalized the purchase, SMI had to sell the Marquette Heights building.

To Ray King, that "seemed like a long shot." About a mile off a state highway on a bluff, and with only one main route into town, it didn't represent a prime business location. But there was one buyer that didn't mind the location: the one-year-old church plant Ted Pittenger called home. Family of Faith needed a building and could pay $265,000.

"That's what we needed to make the whole deal work," Ray said.

A week before the close of the deal, Samaritan leaders made a walk-through of the new building, located in an industrial park in Peoria. While these leaders made their final inspection, the sellers pointed out that office furniture and equipment left in the main building and stored in the warehouse could be thrown away before Samaritan moved in "unless you'd like to have it."

"We thought about it for half a second and said, 'Oh, you can leave it,'" Ray said.

The offer meant desks for private offices and cubicles that might have cost $50,000 or more were already in place. The staff found additional items in the warehouse and donated excess equipment to Peoria Rescue Ministries, which serves homeless men and operates facilities for pregnant women in need in central Illinois.

When moving day arrived in January 2005, Samaritan workers unplugged their phones and computers at the Marquette Heights building, loaded up, moved the equipment to the new building, and by noon the next day were up and running.

"We were able to do that without rewiring or changing much of anything," Ray said. "It was like all the things we needed were already in place. So, again, we thought, 'God just provided for us.'"

However, the Lord wasn't done providing. Through the sale a few years later of an adjacent warehouse that came with their new facility, God provided the resources to create a public policy arm of the ministry to address new challenges that would come—first from various states and then from Congress.

# 7

# IT'S NOT INSURANCE!

As the new millennium wore on, health care sharing by members of Samaritan and other ministries became established as a viable, valued way to do health care apart from insurance. Though not spectacular, growth remained steady. Meanwhile, thanks to Samaritan keeping its noninsurance identity clear, the legal waters proved relatively calm for the ministry.

It helped that most people connected with Samaritan understood what it was—and was not. When asked what impression she had of Samaritan Ministries while growing up as the daughter of SMI's DeWayne Arington, Michelle Arington quickly slapped her knee and loudly proclaimed, "It's not insurance!"

Distinguishing between health care sharing and health insurance is vital to the mission of sharing ministries. This distinction gives HCSMs autonomy to determine what type of needs they will share. States might require insurance companies to cover some medical procedures or services that Christians in HCSMs would find immoral—such as abortion. Other mandates require coverage of treatments that are elective, such as wellness visits, or that stem from unbiblical lifestyles. HCSMs are free to determine what they will and won't share, according to Biblical standards of morality and an emphasis on personal responsibility.

Another reason that health care sharing ministries are not classified as insurance is that they don't keep cash reserves on hand. Health insurance companies are required to maintain contingency funds to assure policyholders they can cover the risks they have assumed. Samaritan doesn't hold the money that is shared among members; the members hold the funds and give them directly to each other.

> Samaritan doesn't hold the money that is shared among members; the members hold the funds and give them directly to each other.

The only time members send money to Samaritan is for annual administrative fees, to contribute to special funds established to help members with extraordinary financial needs, or to help with the ministry's financial needs—such as building expenses or technological upgrades.

The legal battle for health care sharing freedom has primarily occurred at the state level. The Alliance of Health Care Sharing Ministries, which at that time was sponsored by Samaritan, Medi-Share, and Christian Healthcare Ministries (but the impact of which benefits all sharing ministries), has an ongoing effort in states to formally categorize HCSMs apart from insurance. By August 2019, 30 states had passed such "safe-harbor" legislation.[11] Michael Sharman had been instrumental in early initiatives in many of those states, writing legislation that exempted Christian health care sharing from insurance laws. He also won every court challenge at the state level, largely because with HCSMs there is no promise to pay, a distinction that removes it from the realm of insurance.

The lack of member complaints has also helped.

"We're very vulnerable to members having expectations we're going to do this or that," SMI attorney Brian Heller said. However, when people sign up for Samaritan, they agree to not bring legal action against the ministry, a provision based on 1 Corinthians 6:1-8, which admonishes Christians not to take internal grievances to secular courts.

This doesn't mean that Samaritan declines to address member complaints. For example, the Samaritan Guidelines provide for an arbitration process in which a panel of 13 randomly chosen members can hear a member's complaint and reach a binding decision. This helps to defuse many potential lawsuits, and the provision has been invoked only a handful of times. It also helps to have six volunteer Board members elected by members,[12] which gives them even more of a say in SMI operations. Finally, no share increase can occur without members approving it by a 60 percent majority.

The lack of legal action against the ministry, Heller said, also "speaks well of both the members and Member Services representatives."

In other words, sharing ministries can focus more time and energy on helping their members share one another's health care burdens. But legal storms would come—not through the courts, but in state legislatures.

## The "Massachusetts Miracle"

Over the years, Samaritan and other health care sharing ministries had successfully maintained the distinction between themselves and health insurers. For a while, simply keeping a low profile to avoid presenting a convenient target for regulators or a hostile secular news media helped, too.

That luxury ended when two states took action requiring their residents to purchase health insurance.

First, Massachusetts Governor Mitt Romney signed a health care "reform" bill in 2006 that mandated that step. The government policy community in the Bay State had been "frustrated by their inability to control prices" in health care, so "they were looking around for something new to do," according to health care analyst Greg Scandlen. "They seized on the uninsured." That was mainly because politicos had concluded that uncompensated care was driving up the costs of health care. People without the ability to pay were receiving treatment in hospitals, and those hospitals had to get the money from someone—namely, from paying patients.

"So all of a sudden, they pivoted from a concern about cost control to a concern about the uninsured," Scandlen said. "Frankly, I think it was an invented crisis."

The numbers of uninsured Massachusetts residents were relatively modest, sitting at just 9 percent of the state's population at the time the legislature passed the bill.

"But a lot of people who feel like they want to have more control over everything seized on it as an emotional issue," Scandlen said. "That was essentially what Massachusetts did. They completely ignored any kind of cost concern and simply wanted to reduce the numbers of uninsured."

Politicians and policy wonks floated various ideas, like an individual mandate, figuring they could "simply wave their wand and require people to buy insurance and they would have insurance—end of story, problem solved," the analyst said.

Legislators first introduced "An Act Providing Access to Affordable, Quality, Accountable Health Care" in 2004. They passed it the following year, with Romney signing it in 2006. The law included two mandates that would become controversial at a national level by 2009: a requirement for all individuals to purchase insurance, and a requirement that employers with 11 or more employees provide insurance for those workers or pay a penalty. Although Romney vetoed the employer mandate, the legislature overrode the veto in June 2006.

The United States had its first health insurance mandate, which meant that even members of health care sharing ministries in Massachusetts would be required—under state law—to buy insurance. Samaritan leaders started hearing rumblings about other states following Massachusetts's lead. Alarms sounded. Sharing ministries' chief concern had shifted from insurance regulation to mandatory insurance.

James Lansberry and Medi-Share's CEO at the time, Robert Baldwin, flew to Boston and met with lawmakers from an overwhelmingly Democratic legislature. They received little encouragement that they could get an exemption for their members.

Then came the "Massachusetts Miracle."

Brian Heller got the number of a Romney staffer from a Focus on the Family affiliate contact, called the staffer, and explained what HCSMs were and what they did. The staffer's response was, "You do that?" Had they known about health care sharing, the staffer said, they would have tried to get an exemption built into the law—but it was too late.

Although stymied in that effort, Brian learned he should try contacting the new agency overseeing the program to see if SMI could get something inserted into the regulations as they were being written. Brian contacted the agency and left a voice message, doubting whether he would ever hear back. To his surprise, that Friday evening, Brian received a call back from an agency employee. He was very interested and also suggested Brian send information about what HCSMs did. When the regulations appeared, they included an exemption for HCSM members.

"The staffer was our angel that the Lord put in there," Brian said.

In 2007, Samaritan faced the same challenge in Missouri, when a state senator there proposed an individual mandate. "He had bought into some of the misleading ideas about what the uninsured were doing and how much of a problem they really were, and tried to come up with a law," Ray King said.

Ironically, this particular senator knew neither that health care sharing ministries existed as an alternative to insurance, nor that his pastor was a member of Samaritan.

The pastor gave the ministry a heads-up, promoting a meeting between SMI representatives and the senator, who was "basically positive toward us," Ray said. "He was going to legislate us out of existence and not even know he did it."

After they finished their discussion, the legislator directed the Samaritan reps to the chairman of the insurance committee in the Missouri House—a Southern Baptist.

"My, this is really something," the chairman said. "You people . . . you do that? I've never heard of such a thing. That's good. We sure wouldn't want to interfere with that."

These two experiences alerted SMI leaders to the fact that they no longer could afford to "fly under the radar." They needed to gain altitude, publicize their existence, and educate more people about the inner workings of sharing plans.

"We realized that if we didn't get the message out, we'd be regulated out of existence," Ray said. "And so we've gone on kind of the opposite track ever since."

## Call for Help Answered

In order to address public policy challenges from a more proactive stance, Samaritan and Medi-Share forged a cooperative effort to take on legislative threats. The two formed the Alliance of Health Care Sharing Ministries, choosing James Lansberry as president. The Alliance would represent the interests of HCSM members to legislators at both the state and federal levels. Lansberry also led SMI's newly established Public Policy department.

Christian Healthcare Ministries (formerly Brotherhood) was invited but chose not to participate at that time.

In the January 2007 Samaritan newsletter, Ted Pittenger put out a call to the ministry's most valued resource—its members—for help.

"Please first join in fervent prayer for God to intervene in a mighty way," he wrote in his annual State of the Ministry article.

Then he added, "If you are in one of the states where there is a challenge, please let us know how you might be able to join in the battle, and be prepared to make phone calls or join us at your state capitol. If you are in another state, please be alert for similar initiatives there, and let us know what you know and how you might be able to help."

In mid-January, the appeal caught the attention of Joe Guarino, a Samaritan member living in Virginia. Guarino, who had joined Samaritan in 2004, was a lobbyist in Richmond. He knew where to look for legislation, so he checked to see if a Virginia legislator had proposed an individual mandate. Then he called Samaritan to report his findings.

"I said, 'Yes, there's a bill. Oh, by the way, I'm a lobbyist. And, oh, by the way, I'm available if you're looking for help,'" Guarino said.

Lansberry called him back on a Friday and asked if he could visit the home offices for an interview the following Monday. When he made the trip, Guarino unexpectedly faced questioning by seven people.

"I remember thinking, 'This is quite an interview,'" Guarino said. But it was nothing out of the ordinary; Samaritan's leadership team routinely interviewed all prospective employees to make sure they were spiritually sound. Satisfied, SMI immediately hired Joe to handle government affairs at the state level and later at the federal level. He eventually would become a lobbyist for the Alliance of Health Care Sharing Ministries.

Guarino flew to six states in seven months to halt the advance of individual mandates. In late spring of 2007, he started going to Washington, DC, two or three times a month. He continued those trips for the next 18 months, meeting with staffers from about 150 representatives' offices. Those contacts proved invaluable after voters elected Barack Obama as president in November of 2008. Three months later, the new president told a joint session of Congress that he would begin working with legislators to craft a health care "reform" plan.

The national health care battles had resurfaced. Unlike in 1993-94, when a fledgling Samaritan was fighting to get a solid footing (let alone survive a nationalized health care initiative), this time health care sharing ministries were better prepared.

But meeting the next challenges would take fasting, prayer, and harder work than anyone at Samaritan could have imagined.

# MR. LANSBERRY GOES TO WASHINGTON

Even with the encouragement of the Massachusetts Miracle, by early 2009, Samaritan attorney Brian Heller didn't feel overly optimistic about the ministry's future. Looming national health care proposals that would saddle United States citizens with health insurance—whether they wanted it or not—concerned him.

Since Hillary Clinton's effort to nationalize health care in the early 1990s, the industry had changed for both the better and the worse. Insurers had begun to look for a way to make enrollees of their plans behave more like rational consumers, according to Devon Herrick, formerly of the National Center for Policy Analysis. They used several tactics:

- Cost-sharing, which caused deductibles between 1994 and 2004 to nearly double

- A wider variety of health plans—such as managed care and high-deductible plans

- Tiered co-pays for different types of drugs, and penalties for customers making unnecessary visits to the emergency room

- Health savings accounts, medical savings accounts, and flexible spending accounts, which became more common

Meanwhile, the federal government was contravening this trend. Washington had expanded its "cafeteria" of programs, including Medicaid, Medicare, and the Children's Health Insurance Program (widely known as CHIP), the latter initiated under President George W. Bush.

This showdown between a conservative, free-market approach to health care and "progressive," heavy-handed, managed care was inevitable, particularly as health care costs and insurance premiums alike continued their relentless rise over the decade. Indeed, health care was shaping up as a major ideological battleground. The push was on for the federal government to assume unprecedented control in a very personal area of life: medical treatment.

"To a substantial degree, public health advocates who advise members of Congress, Democratic leadership in Congress, and people in Congress who are left of center think there's something fundamentally wrong with reaching for your wallet during a visit to your doctor or a hospital or a pharmacy," Herrick said. "They don't believe health care is a normal market. They don't believe it should be involved in the market process. They simply believe that anything related to cost-sharing or making a decision to get a treatment or not, based on price, is a barrier to access."

After Massachusetts successfully installed its health insurance law in 2006, talk of mandates resurfaced. Like ripples in a pond, plans to enact a large-scale health insurance mandate gradually widened as the 2008 presidential campaign approached.

In an echo of the early 1990s, proponents put forth the idea of an "individual mandate" requiring all US citizens to acquire health coverage of some type, whether private or government. Government could achieve liberals' dream of providing health insurance for all by requiring everyone to buy it. And, if some couldn't afford it, they could just make taxpayers subsidize it.

In the 2008 campaign for the Democratic nomination for president, former First Lady-turned-senator-from-New-York Hillary Clinton (the primary advocate of the 1993-94 universal care scheme) proposed health care "reform." One of its cornerstones: an individual mandate. Another candidate, Illinois Senator Barack Obama, opposed such a mandate. However, once Obama took office, the picture changed. In the spring of 2009, when health care proposals emerging from Congress included an individual mandate, the new president changed his mind.

Under these proposals, health care sharing ministries would face yet another threat. Failure to buy health insurance would result in a fine (which the US Supreme Court later ruled a "tax"). HCSM leaders doubted many of their members could continue to pay their shares if they faced fines for doing so—especially with the amount increasing each year after the law went into effect. Half of Samaritan's membership lived at or below 200 percent of the federal poverty level, with more than 75 percent below the median US family income.

Members of Congress and the Obama administration turned a deaf ear to polls and protests that showed a majority of Americans opposed these left-wing health care proposals. Thus, it became clear the Democrats would pass some version of a health insurance overhaul into law. Needs-sharing ministry leaders realized if they couldn't block an individual mandate, they would need an exemption from it for their members, similar to the one granted in Massachusetts.

Heller warned Samaritan leaders he didn't know how it could happen.

"We're 100,000 little nobodies," he said, referring to the overall number of individuals who belonged to HCSMs at the time. That was practically nothing compared to "huge industries that make campaign contributions."

Then, under James Lansberry's leadership, the Alliance of Health Care Sharing Ministries and Samaritan's Public Policy department made a full-court press to secure an exemption in various legislative proposals. However, they had to move quickly, even when Democrats' mandate-and-penalty agenda suffered a setback—Senate Majority Leader Tom Daschle withdrawing in February 2009 as Obama's nominee to lead the Department of Health and Human Services. The president pressed on despite the loss of Daschle's passion for health insurance reform and political prowess. In March, after a White House forum on health care, Obama vowed to have a plan passed by the end of 2009—then moved the deadline up to August.

But rather than submitting its own plan to a Democrat-controlled Congress, the White House chose to let legislators advance their own proposals. That was a blessing for health care sharing ministries, because it allowed them to work more closely with senators and representatives during the drafting, debate, and amendment of various proposals.

Alliance government affairs consultants Joe Guarino and Martin Hoyt had already been talking to people on Capitol Hill. Joe alone had met with staffers from about 150 US representatives' offices in 2007 and 2008. His reception in those offices was positive for the most part, with only a few displaying antagonistic attitudes toward HCSMs.

"Everybody else was amazed at what we were doing," Joe said.

He pointed out to the congressional staffers that HCSMs weren't giants like Wellpoint or Blue Cross Blue Shield, "but we're also not three or four dozen families in northeastern Kansas trying to do this. We're doing what you desire for everyone to do, and that is to pay their medical bills, so please let us continue," Joe told them.

How could they argue with that?

"Even folks in offices of liberal Democrats did not seem to have much of a problem with us," Joe said later.

That included the office of the main force behind a comprehensive health care law, Senator Ted Kennedy of Massachusetts, whose staff worked with Alliance representatives on including exemption language.

On a Friday afternoon, Hoyt told SMI attorney Brian Heller that Kennedy staffer John McDonough would need proposed exemption language by that next Monday morning.

Heller recalled the process clearly.

"I wish I could say I remember getting down on my knees and praying for wisdom, but in any event, the Holy Spirit gave me the inspiration to look at the legislative language used to exempt the Amish from Social Security," the attorney said. "I thus patterned in part the [Affordable Care Act] exemption language after that. On Monday morning, I sent that language to Marty, who handed it off to Mr. McDonough, and then it showed up virtually identical in the bill."

The one limitation included in the language was a time stamp: the exemption would apply only to members of ministries that had been sharing needs since December 31, 1999, or earlier.

"They didn't want phony entities trying to trick people out of money, sham entities set up to allow people to escape the ACA requirements but not engage in real sharing," Hoyt said.

"We had a limited amount of time to negotiate with Kennedy," Hoyt continued. God also orchestrated support for health care sharing ministries through Republican Senator Charles Grassley of Iowa. Grassley's support was important;

he was a member of the Senate's Gang of Six, a group of three Democrats and three Republicans who worked on compromise health care legislation.

The connection was another one of those "God things." Guarino knew Linda Upmeyer, who at the time was the Republican whip in the Iowa House of Representatives, from his time lobbying at the state level. Grassley was a friend of Upmeyer's father, Del Stromer, who had served as Iowa House Speaker. At Guarino's request, Upmeyer arranged a meeting with Grassley about the exemption. She and three Samaritan members gathered in the legislator's Iowa office for a teleconference. Grassley, Lansberry, Alliance lobbyist Hoyt, and Samaritan staffer Dwayne Carr sat in Grassley's DC office. After delivering the health care sharing message to Grassley, the HCSM proponents suggested language for a sharing ministry exemption. Grassley agreed it was needed and made it a priority in his Gang of Six proceedings. Hoyt said that was one of the reasons it got in the bill.

But inclusion in the Senate Health, Education, Labor, and Pensions Committee's bill, overseen by Kennedy's staff, wasn't enough. Before landing on the Senate floor, a health care reform bill had to make it through the Finance Committee, headed by Senator Max Baucus of Montana, another member of the Gang of Six. A policy paper that had come out of Baucus's office didn't mention religious freedom, but that changed after Hoyt and Guarino approached Baucus and his staff.

"They started making corrections," Hoyt said.

Helping the most was Yvette Fontenot, a Baucus staffer who worked on the Senate Finance Committee.

"She was the critical person to meet to get our language into the Senate Finance bill," Guarino said.

When the text of the bill emerged from committee, it included the proposed language, thanks to its bipartisan support and God's answer to prayer.

Guarino and Hoyt credit God with the Senate successes.

"They were dealing with a huge machine, and we were just a tiny little cog in the middle of all of it that nobody would ever notice," Guarino said.

Hoyt agreed.

"It's a miracle we were there," he said.

Things didn't work out so well on the House side, though. Joe had tried for months to get ahold of a certain staffer on one of the House committees working with Speaker Nancy Pelosi on the House's version of a health care bill. When he finally made contact, the staffer asked, "Aren't you the Christian Scientists?"

House staffers hadn't taken the time to look at sharing ministries and knew nothing about them, except for a few legislators like US Representative Pete Hoekstra of Michigan, who tried to insert exemption language into a House bill at a Health, Employment, Labor, and Pensions Subcommittee meeting that lasted into the wee hours of the morning. At 4:30 a.m. the chairman asked Hoekstra to withdraw his amendment, promising it would be brought back up and put into the bill at a more opportune time. Hoekstra looked at Hoyt, sitting among spectators, and Hoyt nodded his agreement.

"I did not want a negative vote," Hoyt said.

"We knew full well that if Representative Hoekstra said, 'We want this in now,' they had the votes to kill it," Guarino said.

Unfortunately, the chairman didn't keep his promise to revisit the subject, which meant no exemption language made it into any of the House bills under consideration.

As the summer of 2009 progressed, opposition to the Democrats' version of health care reform increased. During the

August recess—which had started without a bill being passed, contrary to Obama's wishes—opponents of the proposals confronted Democratic lawmakers at "town hall" meetings around the nation.[13] With rhetoric ratcheted up, Obama addressed a joint session of Congress on the topic on September 9, calling for action on health care.

While Guarino and Hoyt were working on the legislative front, SMI moved ahead on the spiritual front. Ted Pittenger had called for fasting and prayer among staff members, a call that some members also took up. Samaritan initiated weekly staff prayer sessions (which continue to this day). The ministry urged members to pray for the defeat of the health care bill—or, if it passed, that the final bill contain an exemption for HCSM members. The newsletter and mailings kept members up to date on legislation and action they could take.

A member from Virginia named Chuck Angier wanted to do more than call his congressman. He and his wife, Cathy, visited the congressman, Tom Perriello, a freshman Democrat from Virginia's Fifth Congressional District, and asked him to help health care sharing ministries gain an exemption. Perriello sent a letter supporting an exemption for HCSMs to Speaker Nancy Pelosi and House Majority Leader Steny Hoyer of Maryland.

"A major touchstone of our efforts toward comprehensive healthcare reform has been consumer choice," Perriello wrote. "To that end, individuals who choose to receive their healthcare coverage through health sharing ministries instead of traditional health plans should not be penalized by the tax provisions of the individual mandate."[14]

"That's how far up this went," Guarino said. "This was definitely a team effort. This was not a one-man show at all. We should recognize none of this could have happened without prayer and the actions of a whole team that was working on this."

But an exemption for health care sharing ministries from the mandate tax never was included in the House bill.

Lansberry, meanwhile, pushed the HCSM and health care freedom gospel to the nation. He was a guest on more than five dozen radio programs (some more than once), appearing on the air approximately 100 times. In those mostly friendly interviews, James talked not only about health care sharing ministries and what they offer the Body of Christ, but also about how the pending health care legislation would impinge on religious liberty through its mandates.

Although exemption language had been placed in the Senate bill, its absence from the House bill meant it still had the potential to be lost once the two pieces of legislation were combined in a conference committee. That meant that in the first week of November 2009, when rumors began to circulate that the House was getting ready to bring a bill to the floor for debate and a vote, the Alliance—and Samaritan staff and members—had to switch into high gear.

## Taking to the Phones

Monday, November 2, arrived amid rumors of a possible vote a day or two later. So, Samaritan's Public Policy and Systems departments created a plan. Volunteers would stay after hours—without pay—and call members who lived in districts represented by members of Congress whose vote was uncertain.

The calls started late that afternoon, with staffers using lists of members within a specific area. Armed with contact information for representatives' offices, staffers asked members to call their congressional representatives and urge them to vote against the health care bill if it didn't contain an exemption for HCSM members. The normal buzz of voices in Samaritan's

Member Services area doubled in intensity, thanks to two dozen people working the phones there and in the adjacent Communications area. Many members said they had already urged their representative to vote against the health care bill on principle and would call them again. The calls continued for a few hours. When staffers completed their lists, they returned to the Systems department for more names and numbers. One snag required a lot of redialing: Samaritan had only two dozen outgoing lines, fewer than the number of staffers who had volunteered to call. Someone trying to get a line out had to punch the "9" key several times.

The rumors of an impending vote, though, turned out either to be false or premature. Not that it mattered much. The evening had served as a dry run for the following Saturday, November 7. By that time, it had become clear that Speaker Nancy Pelosi would gavel the House into session for debate and a vote on that chamber's version of health care reform.

James Lansberry, heading home from a road trip that morning, had heard that the votes of 40 representatives were still unknown or uncertain. He called Samaritan Systems staffer Seth Ben-Ezra, who was also his neighbor in Peoria. James told him that Samaritan needed to put together another call list quickly. Volunteers needed to make contact with members in key districts to again ask them to urge their representatives to vote against any bill that didn't contain a health care sharing exemption. They also asked members to urge their representatives to offer an employer exemption amendment that would include health care sharing participation as an acceptable, credible option for employers and employees.

When James arrived, Seth tried to set up shop at James Lansberry's house but couldn't get his laptop to work on the Lansberrys' Wi-Fi connection, so they walked back down to

Ben-Ezra's home. Despite connection problems there, too, James would end up getting online through his mobile phone.

Meanwhile, a normal Saturday had turned upside down in Bryan Evans' rural home in Hopedale, about half an hour from Peoria. Joining Bryan—the SMI Treasurer and Systems Chief at the time—were his son, Colton (also a Systems employee), and John Creath, a Member Services Specialist who had previously worked in the Public Policy department. At the time, John, his wife, Whitney, and their children lived in a trailer on the Evanses' property. John was in the middle of making home repairs that day and was about to grab a late lunch when the call came from Lansberry. After failing to create an acceptable war room in the Creath trailer, the three men moved to Bryan's home office, where they joined Lansberry and Ben-Ezra in a conference call.

By 11:30, the group agreed that the Peoria crew would assemble the call list and scripts, while Hopedale would stay in touch with staffers who agreed to give up a couple hours of their Saturday to make calls to members. The respective teams then sprang into action.

"There were definitely a lot of moving parts," Colton Evans remembered.

Most staffers contacted agreed to make the calls, although some couldn't because they lacked internet access at home and therefore couldn't receive the call lists electronically. Others had family commitments, while one person's name was automatically eliminated because he was a seventh-day Sabbath keeper.

John Creath had laid most of the groundwork, calling the offices of congressional representatives to see if they were open. (He called them directly, because the Capitol switchboard is closed on weekends). Some were open; some closed offices left alternate numbers on their voice mails. And some were simply unreachable. Having all this information handy saved much time.

Many Samaritan staffers went above and beyond the call of duty. One example is DeWayne Arington, then attending a Bible Bowl quiz meet in Indianapolis with his family. He received his lists on his mobile phone as PDF files and made the calls from the quiz site.

"There were many sacrifices that day," Colton said.

Roger Heffner, a team leader in Member Services, was about two hours away from Peoria, returning from a visit to his family in Ohio, when Bryan Evans reached him. When Roger arrived home, he printed out the list sent to him via email and made calls while he watched Ohio State beat Penn State 16–7.

Attorney Brian Heller was at that weekend's Washington Community High School state playoff football game when his phone rang for the initial conference call. After making some calls from the game, he went back to his nearby office and made more. Having drawn Ohio Representative Dennis Kucinich's district, he found out that the congressman's office was answering the phones and that he had plenty of time to make his calls. He reached seven of the nine members on his list; each one expressed appreciation for the call and promised to contact the representative immediately.

"I found the experience encouraging—that such a high percentage of our members were at least on the surface willing to interrupt their day and make such a call, and no one was upset at having their day interrupted," Heller said. In all, more than 20 Samaritan staffers called members in more than 35 congressional districts. Staffers reported to the Hopedale crew about their success in contacting members, as the color scheme on a shared Google spreadsheet started showing more greens (success) than reds (failure).

Families, as always, helped out. Whitney Creath and Kim and Grace Evans (Bryan's wife and daughter, respectively) prepared potato soup and homemade bread for John, Bryan, and Colton for lunch that day and delivered it to the team.

The Peoria crew wrapped up business by late afternoon. Seth Ben-Ezra, who still had to host a birthday party for one of his sons, headed upstairs with his own call sheets and a phone. Though mentally exhausted, he appreciated the nature of the "all-hands-on-deck" situation.

"Part of it is, it's your salary that's at stake, but also it's really important for a lot of people," Seth said.

By around 6:00 p.m., the crews had completed their calls. Now came the waiting game.

Later that night, the Ben-Ezras and the Lansberrys watched House proceedings together on C-SPAN. House Resolution 3962, "to provide affordable, quality health care for all Americans," lacked that crucial exemption from the individual mandate for health care sharing ministries. The House passed the measure by a 220–215 vote at 11:16 p.m. (EST). A change of only three votes would have altered the outcome.

"I had a lot of mixed feelings," Ben-Ezra said. "We made this massive push, and it seemed like it didn't work, but that really isn't true. It was really close, and who knows how much influence our effort actually had?"

Despite the disappointment, Seth felt pleased with how Samaritan leaders, staffers and, most of all, members had come together for what Colton Evans called "a collective effort to save this ministry" in such a short time.

"It's something I would have pitched in to help another ministry do for free," Colton said. "That was the spirit of a lot of people that day."

Lansberry was "really impressed with how the staff banded together."

"I thought the devotion of our staff to pull together at the last minute and to act for the sake of the members and to encourage members to call was really encouraging," the executive vice president said. "It was a really neat thing to see."

## God Moves—Again

The House of Representatives outcome of November 7 represented only half the battle. Action remained on the Senate bill, which included HCSM exemption language. SMI staff and members continued fasting and praying the language would survive. God answered those prayers. On Christmas Eve 2009, the Senate bill passed 60–39 on a straight party-line vote. Even then, the battle continued. Success would come only if the bill that emerged from a conference committee retained the exemption language—far from a sure thing. It appeared intense negotiations lay ahead; among other things, the Senate bill lacked a "public option"—in essence, a government-run health insurance agency that would compete with privately owned agencies. Senator Joe Lieberman, an independent from Connecticut, had threatened to block a vote on any health care bill that contained a public option. The House bill included this option, a long-standing dream of liberal backers of health care reform. Reconciling the two bills lay in murky, uncertain waters.

The question became moot on January 19, 2010, when Massachusetts voters surprised the nation. Despite their liberal bent, voters chose Republican Scott Brown to fill the Senate seat left vacant the previous August by Senator Ted Kennedy's death. While leaning left on certain social issues, Brown had vowed to oppose the health care bill, which in some ways was to serve as the crowning achievement of Kennedy's career. The Senate bill had come out of the Health, Education, Labor, and Pensions Committee, which Kennedy had chaired for many years. Not surprisingly, the bill contained language favored by Kennedy. But with Brown's upset election over Massachusetts Attorney General Martha Coakley, the Democrats lost the 60 sure votes they needed to end filibusters.

That meant Democrats who backed one of the differing bills passed by the House and Senate had to find another way to get a bill to President Obama's desk. They managed through a parliamentary maneuver. After abandoning a "deem-and-pass" strategy, in which House majority leadership would have "deemed" the Senate bill to have passed without an actual vote, Democrats settled on a "reconciliation" approach.

On March 21, 2010, the House voted 220–211 to pass, in essence, the Senate bill. The legislation survived only after liberal Democrats gave up their insistence on a government-funded public option, and after pro-life Democrats, led by Representative Bart Stupak of Michigan, gained President Obama's assurances that the health care bill would not provide government funding of abortions. Pro-lifers called Obama's executive order to implement that promise "useless," because executive orders cannot override a law, and any president can change an executive order at any time.

So, two days later, Barack Obama signed a form of the law he had sought for a year, albeit a flawed version. The results were bittersweet for Samaritan, too. The exemption from the individual insurance mandate stayed alive thanks to much prayer, fasting, and effort. It also survived thanks to the parliamentary maneuvering that prohibited House members from offering amendments to the Senate bill. That meant the exemption—buried deep inside the 2,400-page legislation—couldn't get stripped away. Although Christians could continue to share each other's health care burdens, Congress had passed a law that would make obtaining quality, reasonably priced health care more difficult for most Americans.

## Another Memorial Stone Put in Place

The inclusion of an exemption for HCSM members in the Affordable Care Act isn't the only example of God reminding Samaritan Ministries of His involvement in the ministry's efforts.

Samaritan attorney Brian Heller calls God's intervention in these situations, each of which could have sunk or seriously harmed Samaritan, "memorial stones." Such markers reflect God's command to each leader of the tribes of Israel to place a stone from the Jordan at the lodging place near where God stopped the waters for Israel to cross the river (Joshua 4:1-7).

One stone, Brian believes, was the avoidance of any overwhelming needs in SMI's early days. Another was securing for HCSM members an exemption from Massachusetts' health care mandate, followed by the federal exemption.

A fourth stone started rolling on April Fool's Day 2011. The state of Washington suddenly imposed a cease-and-desist order (CDO) on Samaritan Ministries, demanding a halt to any needs-sharing activities involving their residents. The state's Insurance Commission took the action after hearing about Samaritan from a television news crew. Ironically, not one Washingtonian had ever filed a complaint about SMI.

"It so came out of the blue," Ted Pittenger said. "When other states would ask us, 'What are you guys doing?' we'd send them information about the ministry and never hear from them again. Washington didn't even call us."

Three days later, the ministry emailed all members living in Washington to inform them about the order, ask for prayer, and appeal for any information that would help SMI respond effectively.

A reaction came quickly.

The next morning's responses from members included one from Jeff Baxter, who had been appointed as a state senator just four weeks before Washington issued its CDO. Another came from a longtime political strategist and lobbyist named Doug Simpson. "By coincidence," Simpson would be at the Washington State Capitol in Olympia that month to lobby for an unrelated bill. Both Baxter and Simpson helped with the goal of a legislative solution to avoid expensive litigation.

As Ray King wrote in the June 2011 newsletter, "God's timing is perfect."[15] Further evidence of that came in the form of a bill backed by the state's insurance commissioner—whose office had issued the CDO—to coordinate Washington's health care laws with new federal bills. The state's upper chamber had already passed the bill, and the lower chamber had undertaken amendments to the proposal. That same week in April, the Washington House passed an amendment to that health care bill, to which the insurance commissioner did not object. That amendment stated that health care sharing ministries are not insurance, thereby exempting them from Insurance Commission regulations. The House returned the legislation to the Senate, which also passed it. Governor Chris Gregoire signed the bill into law on May 11, just 40 days after regulators issued the CDO. Thanks to this divine timing, Samaritan members in Washington didn't miss a beat in sharing needs for April or May.

Thanks to this divine timing, Samaritan members in Washington didn't miss a beat in sharing needs for April or May.

"In the end it is amazing to us that an effort to restrict health care sharing actually resulted in greater protection for the ministry in a state where we were not seeking such protection," Ray wrote.[16]

Fascinated with the process taking exactly 40 days, Ted Pittenger couldn't help thinking of a saying he heard several years earlier: "Forty, but 41's coming." Forty, of course, is a common Biblical number: The Israelites wandered for 40 years in the wilderness; Moses spent 40 days on Mount Sinai when receiving the Torah; Jesus fasted in the wilderness for 40 days at the beginning of His ministry. Thus, the idea that 40 symbolizes a time of preparation, "but 41's coming." Ted even applied that to the timing of Samaritan's blossoming as a ministry. He reached 40 years of age in 1995, when Samaritan's future was in doubt, but after turning 41 the next year, membership rose, and the future looked bright.

Yet another stone came into place in 2012, when Kentucky's Department of Insurance (DOI) moved to halt sharing by the Florida-based health care sharing ministry, Medi-Share, claiming it operated too much like insurance. Samaritan immediately offered to accept Medi-Share's Kentucky members until the other ministry could resolve the situation. Shortly thereafter, the Kentucky DOI asked to meet with representatives of, first, Samaritan and, later, Christian Healthcare Ministries.

Samaritan's meeting didn't start well. Ted, James Lansberry, and Brian Heller sat across the table from the state's insurance commissioner, an assistant, and two attorneys.

"I'm thinking, 'Oh my goodness, we've walked into an inquisition,'" Ted remembered.

One attorney was "like a pit bull with a chip on his shoulder, looking for some reason to nail us to the wall."

The state's representatives started asking questions, but James handled them with aplomb. A big objection appeared to be that members would be kicked out if they couldn't pay their shares (apparently forgetting that insurance companies were free to do just that to customers who didn't pay premiums). James told them about a couple who had stopped paying shares right before the wife was diagnosed with brain cancer. Samaritan helped them meet all their expenses anyway.

"That deflated the attorney," Ted said.

The insurance commissioner's attitude changed from, "We're going to get you guys" to "Oh, wow, you guys really are pretty charitable, aren't you?" Ted said.

Ultimately, the existing safe-harbor law protecting health care sharing ministries was amended to clarify protection. Medi-Share and other HCSMs were able to continue sharing needs with residents of that state.

## The Good, the Bad, and the Media

Although health care sharing ministries through the grace of God survived the Affordable Care Act, the law is "a very dangerous thing for the health care industry and for Americans in general," James Lansberry says. Samaritan and other HCSMs favor the freedom of Americans to make their own health care choices; the ACA limited those choices. An individual mandate, even one with an exemption for HCSM members, stifles choice—Americans would be able to choose only health insurance that the government deemed acceptable. There also is concern that various aspects of the health care law (the provisions of which still face various legal and practical hurdles) will lead to increased medical costs, meaning increases for HCSM members as well.

On the other hand, Lansberry said, "There are some things economically in there that may actually increase favorability toward cash-paying patients."

Another advantage given to HCSM members by the new health care law has been the assurance that, as members of a ministry, none of their money would go toward abortion or treatment of illnesses caused by unbiblical lifestyles. That may be one reason for Samaritan's membership surge right after President Obama signed the health insurance law in March 2010. Over the next 10 months, Samaritan saw then-record growth of 1,900 households, boosting membership to 16,300 households. Another reason for growth may have been Samaritan's higher media profile. After the Affordable Care Act became law, news outlets took notice of the exemption.

In a few cases, coverage proved hostile, focusing on the ministry's refusal to share bills related to abortions or illnesses resulting from unbiblical lifestyles. In other cases, such as a June 2010 story in *Time* magazine, reporters tried hard to grasp the concept but failed to give a clear explanation. Secular media marveled over how Christians could just trust strangers to send them enough money to pay their medical bills.

Some suggested the ministries were being used for political purposes. For instance, in March 2011, *Dan Rather Reports*—a cable news show hosted by the former *CBS Evening News* anchorman—tied health care sharing's growing reputation as an "alternative" to the Affordable Care Act to "political motives." And, like many other reports of that time, it prominently featured criticism by state insurance commissioners.

As time went on, though, media coverage improved.

"There's a level at which the language in the Affordable Care Act gives us just slightly more credibility," Lansberry said. "There's been less going out of their way to show how 'these poor, unregulated companies are going to take advantage of people and make their life horrible, and how we need to make sure that we regulate them so they can't hurt people,' and a lot more of 'Wow, this is a great idea.'"

Lansberry attributes some of that improvement to members who are doing a good job of explaining why they like being part of Samaritan or other HCSMs and how it fulfills their expectations.

One thing had become clear through the experience, though. God was working on behalf of Samaritan and religious liberty. The unlikely legislative scenario that unfolded is proof.

"God does honor our prayers," James Lansberry said after the president signed the health care bill. "He wants us to turn to Him, and I think the mere fact that we see this exemption is obviously an answer to prayer. There's no plan that we could have devised that would have gotten that language into the bill. Yet God had prepared beforehand this way for us to see that language come into the bill and protect these ministries. It was completely from the hand of God."

# 9

# "A BETTER WAY TO DO THINGS"

Health care sharing is counterintuitive. After all, there are no guarantees. In its place comes trust . . . trust in God and the Body of Christ. Longtime members insist this is a better way of taking care of health care needs.

Illinois member Robert Rutan said he and his wife, Kelly, joined despite the lack of a guarantee from SMI that their needs would be met. Their faith proved reliable, with their needs met even in the face of steep medical expenses for cancer treatments.

"We know the stability and the dependability of the members," Kelly said.

And it's a "more responsible way to manage our own health," she added, referring to the freedom Samaritan grants her to visit whichever health care providers her family chooses. Still, participation in a health care sharing ministry includes responsibilities. Members must learn to negotiate lower charges for medical services, something people with health insurance rarely think about. But when you're responsible for how much money other brothers and sisters in Christ will have to send, you become more aware of what you're spending, whether it's necessary, and whether the treatment is available elsewhere for a lower cost.

That freedom to choose and the encouragement to take responsibility for one's choices impresses Grace-Marie Turner.

Turner is founder and president of The Galen Institute, a public policy research organization focused on health care. During a visit to Samaritan headquarters in 2010, she said the ministry is "a really wonderful example of giving people the option to make their own decisions about health care and to be responsible in their health spending, as well as their consumption of health care overall."

"It's a community of people who know they are sharing the costs together, and those costs are visible to them," she said. "I think it's absolutely a model for what the rest of the health care system needs to learn: a community of people who exercise individual responsibility in taking care of themselves and their family and also who recognize that any excess spending on their part increases health care costs for the whole community. We don't have that in the rest of the health care sector."

Jason Morris, former Member Services Manager and now Director of Member Experience and Strategic Relationships, echoed Turner.

"It's a better way to do things," he said. "There's the community element [and] personal responsibility."

Jason said he took "great pleasure" in walking into a hospital after the birth of one of his daughters and paying a $7,000 bill with the cash he received from other members. He had two goals in mind, starting with wanting to see the dollars the hospital charged (which he called unreasonable). Secondly, he wanted to show this provider that insurance isn't an indispensable element of health care.

"We had help, but there's still that sense of, 'I was responsible for this even though you didn't think I was going to be,'" Jason said. "There's something liberating about that."

As attorney Brian Heller points out, "It's a witness to the world and a call to the true Christian believers, saying, 'Hey, there is a way to live more Biblically and faithfully, whether it's tithing or not going into debt—those kinds of Biblical principles that are hard for the average American to live out.'"

One of the challenges of issuing that call to Americans is explaining what Samaritan Ministries *is* rather than what it *isn't*.

> "We've found ourselves over the years explaining what we **aren't** more than what we **are**," Ray King said.

"We've found ourselves over the years explaining what we *aren't* more than what we *are*," Ray King said. "People ask, 'What do you do?' And we say, 'Well, we're not this and we don't do this, and we don't have premiums.' People will ask, 'Well, what do you cover?' Well . . . we don't cover anything."

Samaritan is always learning how to convey what it does in a world that doesn't understand "and can't even relate to the approach we take," Ray said. "When we explain why we're not insurance and not promising to do anything, it sounds even more undependable."

When representing Samaritan at a trade show or conference and someone asks what SMI does, Ray responds that it's a way "for Christians to help each other with health care needs without using health insurance."

"Our message has been that God is more dependable than anyone else," Ray said. "He's where we should be putting our faith for our health care needs. When we try to be independent of God, we don't get to experience His care."

## Shifting One's Paradigm

The health care sharing concept is still hard for many Christians to assimilate. Although it has a relatively short lifespan in the annals of the nation's history, health insurance still maintains a stranglehold on the minds of most Americans (including Christians). General Counsel Brian Heller said dependence on insurance is "so built into the American thought process that it takes a jolt to get people out of that, even if they're intrigued by health care sharing." Sometimes it takes an individual mandate forcing Americans to buy health insurance to make people question the norm. Whether gradual or sudden, it can take a price increase in the worker's share of premiums to open some people's eyes. Others experience an awakening after starting their business and facing sole responsibility for health care premiums. Sometimes a working mom whose job pays in health benefits will decide it's better to stay at home with her growing children than remain in the workforce; when she quits her job, coverage ceases.

At first, however, health care sharing is often "so out of people's realm of thinking that it doesn't even register," Ted Pittenger said. "I'm sure it's like homeschooling was when it revived in the 1980s. People said, 'You're going to do what? Public education seems to be working okay.' It's just such a weird paradigm shift."

Bob and Kelly Rutan were in the midst of such a shift when they joined Samaritan in 2002. Bob was on his way out of the public school system, where he had taught for several years.

"It wasn't hard to understand how [health care sharing] works, once you have thoroughly examined it and understand how everything should work," Bob said. "It takes a commitment to understand a new way of thinking. Once I did, it was easy for us."

It wasn't easy for extended family, though. His parents, and Kelly's, expressed concern that such a ministry would fail to adequately meet their expenses. They finally stopped fretting when shares fully paid for one of Kelly's childbirths.

"They don't know how it all works, but they know that it worked," Bob said.

Another family, David and Lisa Gordon of the state of Washington, joined Samaritan in January 2011 even while still wondering "if this really works." Then, after sending shares to other members for 18 months, one of their daughters needed treatment for skin issues, and the Gordons had to submit their first need.

"The process was very simple," Lisa said in a July 2012 letter. "We have been so blessed by seeing our financial need met by other members and [having] our daughter lifted up in prayer. And the answer to our question at the beginning of our membership is . . . 'Yes!' Samaritan works."

Ted said he can't be too hard on Christians who don't accept the health care sharing way of handling medical expenses. He points to the marketing adage that people need seven exposures to a new idea before they embrace it. Samaritan leaders are also patient when it comes to the Body of Christ understanding the advantages of health care sharing, because they understand God works in His own good time. And they see their work as God's work, since health care sharing—and the prayer and expressions of love that accompany it—are ways to further The Kingdom of God.

Ted, who, along with Ray King, closes his letters with "For The Kingdom," says, "In a sense, we're literally taking back the earth through the dominion mandate of taking ground for Jesus. We're spreading His Kingdom here on earth. It says in Psalms that the earth will be His footstool. I see what we're doing at Samaritan Ministries as furthering His Kingdom, furthering His dominion in the world."

## Taking Back Health Care Charity

As a Kingdom effort, Samaritan has always taken a strong pro-life stance. From the beginning, Samaritan made it clear that members would not be asked to share expenses for any unbiblical medical procedures, such as abortion.

"I think initially our general stand was that bad lifestyle choices make for a lot of medical expenses," Ted said. "I was told early on that 70 percent of medical needs come from bad lifestyle choices. When you eliminate most of those bad lifestyle choices with a group of committed Christians, it's not surprising that you would also have lower costs."

Such an approach dovetails with James Lansberry's emphasis on the need for the Church to take back health care charity.

"I think charity belongs to the Church in the sense that this is something we're supposed to be doing for Jesus's name," he said.

The Church allowed the government to take over a large part of its charitable health care work with the onset of Medicare and Medicaid in the mid-1960s. While many hospitals still bear Christian-oriented names or denominational backers, "half of their bottom line comes from federal funds through Medicare and Medicaid."

"We've allowed that to be the reason for government to take care of the elderly and to take care of the sick instead of it being something that we do," Lansberry said. That's one of the reasons Lansberry and the ministry started the Morning Center—to provide free, quality maternity care for needy pregnant women. (See chapter 14 for more on the Morning Center.)

It is also why Samaritan is the only one of the four largest ministries (if you include Liberty Healthshare) that explicitly discourages members from going to Medicaid or CHIP for assistance with medical expenses.

Charging for health care services is "certainly legitimate," but when people who need health care grapple with difficult financial circumstances, the Church should provide those services in Jesus's name, James continued.

"When you're receiving taxpayer dollars for it, it undermines the ability of us to minister for the glory of Jesus," he said. "Our Father has not run out of money. God owns the cattle on a thousand hills. His riches make Bill Gates and Warren Buffett look like paupers. We forget how many riches we have in Christ. We don't need money. We need people who are willing to stand up and do what we're supposed to do, which is to do good for others in Jesus's name. That's really what charity is. It's doing good to others in Jesus's name at a sacrifice to ourselves. We've lost that willingness to sacrifice, and we need to take that back."

# 10

# HOW HEALTH CARE SHARING WORKS

Since it is far removed from health insurance, Samaritan Ministries' sharing process can appear confusing at first. Joining the SMI family (or any other sharing plan) requires shifting from society's accepted paradigm for meeting health care needs.

Once someone experiences it, though, the concept seems simple.

Inquiries from prospective members and curiosity seekers follow a consistent pattern. Vice President of External Relations Anthony Hopp says the following are among the frequently asked questions fielded by Membership Development staff. Their replies follow in italics:

- Is this insurance? *No.*

- What's the cost? *Depends on your household size.*

- What does it "cover"? *We don't cover anything; we share.*

- How long have you guys been around? *Since 1994.*

- How many members are there? *As of November 2019, more than 82,000 households.*

- How are you different from Medi-Share and Christian Healthcare Ministries? *Mainly in the way we share needs and what we will share.*

- What about needs over $250,000? *You need to be in Save to Share to have an amount over $250,000 shared.*

- What about pre-existing conditions? *Some may be submitted to our Member Assistance Fund. Others may qualify if there's a certain time period without symptoms or treatment.*

- Are the shares I receive taxable income? *So far, the IRS has not treated share amounts received as taxable income.*

- Are the shares I send deductible on my taxes? *Ask your tax professional.*

- What about prescriptions? *They're shared on a limited basis if they're related to a need.*

- Are maternity needs published? *Yes.*

- How soon can I get started? Is there a waiting period? *No. Just submit a properly completed application.*

- Are you guys accountable to anyone? *To our members and a Board of Directors, two-thirds of whom are elected by the members, as well as the Internal Revenue Service and state attorneys general, who have oversight of charities.*

- What happens if there are more medical needs than shares available? *We prorate for that month.*

- What happens if there are more shares than medical needs presented? *Usually some needs are paid early; more rarely, share amounts are reduced for a month.*

- What is the turnaround time for a medical need to be shared? *Between 30 and 60 days from the time a bill is properly submitted.*

- Is there a lifetime, per person, or per year dollar maximum? *No. Just a per need maximum of $250,000 per incident for* *those who aren't in Save to Share. For those in Save to Share, there is no maximum.*

- What happens if someone doesn't send his or her share? *We see what the situation is with the person who didn't send the share. Eventually, we may need to share that amount with other members.*

- Is there a minimum time I need to be a member to have a need shared? *No.*

- Can I cancel at any time? *Yes.*

- This sounds a little scary and pie-in-the-sky. Does it really work? *Yes.*

Membership starts with an application that includes agreement to a basic statement of faith in God and verification by a church leader (pastor, deacon, elder, officer, etc.) that the applicant(s) follow a Biblical lifestyle. Once a household joins, SMI mails monthly share slips to the member. The assigned share amount depends on several factors:

- Size of household. SMI breaks down share levels according to the number of people who are members. The levels are one person, two persons (e.g., a husband and wife, parent and child, or two siblings), a single parent and one or more children, and a family of two parents and one or more children.

- A member's age. Heads of household age 29 years or younger are assigned a reduced share.

- Membership level: Samaritan Classic features higher sharing levels but shares more of a need; Samaritan Basic has lower sharing levels, but the member is responsible for more of a need.

- Membership in Save to Share. The ministry shares up to $250,000 per need. To have amounts beyond that limit shared, a member must join Save to Share. This add-on program involves agreeing to set aside an extra amount per year, again depending on household size. How much of that amount a Save to Share member will share (out of the set-aside amount) varies month to month, depending on the Save to Share needs for a particular month.

Each month, Samaritan sends each member household a copy of the newsletter, along with a prayer guide, a share slip telling the household how much its share is for the month (it can vary for members of Save to Share), whom to send their share to, and how to pray for that person.

Once a member has a need, his or her involvement in the sharing process changes, beginning with a call to Member Services (MS) to let an advocate know about the need. This advocate serves as the member's representative, helping him or her resolve a need or other situation involving membership. The advocate's job doesn't stop with updating a database or staying on top of paperwork. Once most members have joined Samaritan, Member Services will be their only contact point with the ministry. Whether they have a need to be shared, a question about some aspect of their membership, or a problem keeping up with membership, they call MS.

A good MS specialist is "someone who can do a lot of repetitive, mundane things," said Micah Repke, a longtime Member Services staffer. "Someone who can roll with the punches."

Most new MS reps have both a procedural and spiritual learning curve. They never know from one minute to another what kind of call or email they will receive.

"You could get one phone call in which a member was just diagnosed with cancer or has a loved one in the hospital with some problem, or even has lost a loved one," Micah said. "Maybe they're changing churches and they're going through a really difficult time. You pray with that person and you empathize with that person. And the next phone call, seconds later, a person is ecstatic about a big discount or a healing. Sometimes you're even dealing with a difficult situation in which a member is lashing out, or is dissatisfied, or is angry at the medical provider." MS specialists must find a balance between being able to empathize with and encourage members, but not take the weight of the job home with them.

> MS specialists must find a balance between being able to empathize with and encourage members, but not take the weight of the job home with them.

"We don't want our people to be cold and unsympathetic," Micah said. "We want them to pray for our members and identify with them. But sometimes you need a break, so as not to make members' issues your issues."

MS advocates are the ones who give initial direction to need processing by checking the Guidelines and informing need processors to send paperwork to a member. They also compose the prayer request related to a need that will find its way into an upcoming prayer guide.

However, this applies only to incidents over the minimum threshold, which as of mid-2019 was $1,500 for the Samaritan Basic membership level and $300 for the Samaritan Classic membership level. Anything under those amounts—typically for preventive care or minor illnesses—depending on membership level, is not shared. If it is over that amount, the need is "created" in the database, as is a prayer request. The MS advocate then prays with the member about the need and situation—something that would likely never take place with a health insurance company.

"Prayer is a big part of it for the member advocates," said Cameron Easley, Samaritan's Member Services Director.

Members enjoy this personal care. Their letters to the home office routinely mention how much they appreciate being able to pray with a Member Services advocate.

Repke said he has encouraged team members to "put a lot of effort into our prayer requests: keeping them up to date, making sure that an accurate prayer request is written." For instance, if a member gets test results back, he or she typically lets MS know so someone can write a prayer update.

After a need is created by phone, a need processing form goes out to the member, along with instructions on collecting bills and forms from doctors, hospitals, clinics, and other health care providers. If the need is created online, through the Samaritan Dashboard, then images of bills are submitted and forms filled out.

Once the forms and bills are in Samaritan hands, a data validator enters the information into the database and files the forms. An MS specialist then checks the information, making sure the member has properly filled out the need processing form and itemized the bills. Once approved, the need is set up to share, and a needs status notification goes out. That lets the member know if there are any problems with the need, which bills are shareable, and roughly when the need will be published.

## Detours of a Need

This process can take a couple detours, though.

For instance, MS may determine that a need doesn't fall within the approved Guidelines. The need may be related to a pre-existing condition, like diabetes or cancer, or something that simply isn't included in the sharing program, like orthodontic or dental work. If a final determination of whether a need can be shared is required, that usually goes to MS Director Cameron Easley.

The lanky, easygoing Easley is about the last person you'd expect to be hardnosed, but when the answer to whether a need can be shared through the regular route is "no," he will say so.

"My job is to be the jerk," Cameron says. "I'm the one who has to tell the members 'no.'"

When MS reps bring a case to Cameron, they will act as advocates for the members, arguing their case to get a need shared. *Why can't we do this? Can't we stretch the Guidelines a little bit here?*

Sometimes, though, even if Guidelines applications are pretty clear, being told "no" doesn't sit well with a member. Such cases wind up on Cameron's desk.

"When they say, 'Can I talk to your manager?,' I'm the guy they come to in that situation," he says.

Being declined from sharing medical expenses as a regular need doesn't necessarily mean the end of the story. Often, the expenses can be shared as what has traditionally been called a Special Prayer Need (SPN). Members are not expected to send money for SPNs, but they are encouraged to voluntarily send an extra gift directly to the member or through the Member Assistance Fund.

SPNs start "like any other need," Cameron said, but take a detour when an MS advocate determines that the need doesn't fall within the Guidelines. The most frequent type of SPN is dental work, which typically isn't shareable as a regular need unless related to an injury or other medical situation. Other examples of SPNs are ongoing medication, supplies for pre-existing conditions like diabetes or sleep apnea, and routine procedures like colonoscopies or mammograms. The MS advocate will let the member know the need isn't a regular need but might qualify for member assistance.

Determining whether a need can become an SPN depends on "such criteria as the extent of the financial burden, the availability of assistance from other sources, the degree to which the need was avoidable, and the amount of other pending requests."[17]

If staffers determine that a need qualifies, it goes to an MS manager, who files the Needs on a first-come, first-served basis. A specific gift is suggested to members for SPNs each month, depending on the SPN amounts for that month. A certain minimum number of households, as well as a small percentage over that number, are asked to consider helping out the member with the SPN. The idea is that if everyone sent the suggested amount, the need would be met.

In all cases, SMI encourages prayers for members' medical and financial needs. Cameron estimated that those with SPNs typically get 30 percent of what they request.

"The members understand they are going to have to pay that out of their own pocket, but having the Body of Christ being able to set aside extra funds—30 bucks a month or so—to help people for whatever reason their need isn't publishable—it's just an extra way of helping," Cameron said.

Member Rita Hatfield of West Virginia was grateful for such help.

"I thought, 'How many would respond to my need?'" Rita wrote to the ministry. "I knew my need was not publishable; it would take people with a kind heart and an understanding of how hard it is to have such a financial burden. I never dreamed

I would receive so many responses. I was overwhelmed, humbled, and excited. My husband and I were so excited to go to the mailbox."

Rita received 162 cards or letters from people in 31 states. In a "widow's mite" action, one woman who didn't have a job or a house still sent a gift, Rita reported.

While some non-Christians may scoff at the idea of health care sharing and Christians voluntarily sending money to other Christians, the Special Prayer Needs process alone shows they are wrong. SPNs are identified as opportunities for Samaritan members to go above and beyond their regular sharing. They are included on the monthly share slip with a note reading, "A small additional gift can help make a big difference."

It does.

"It is my belief that my Special Prayer Need is the best example of Christian benevolence in action," member Pete Ernst wrote in 2010 after one of his SPNs was included on a share slip. "I was amazed to go to my mailbox and find enormous checks from people who hadn't even made any faith commitment to give to my need but were led to give by the Holy Spirit."

Paul Perryman, who joined Samaritan in 2015, not long after racking up nearly $100,000 in bills incurred by a triathlon accident, received $24,000 in Special Prayer Need donations from members.

"To me, this is the Body of Christ working together the way it should," he said. "People who will never see me or know me this side of Heaven sent money to help with my medical need."

## Negotiating Medical Bills

Before sharing regular needs, SMI makes an effort to reduce the amount of the bills. Sometimes the member handles that job by simply asking a health care provider for a self-pay discount. Alternatively, negotiators from The Karis Group (TKG) or Advanced Medical Pricing Solutions (AMPS) will get involved.

Medical billing has been compared to the "rack rate" on the back of a hotel room's door, a price that is usually much higher than any guest will ever pay, or the sticker price on a car, which everybody knows won't be the final price. TKG calls the medical sticker price a "hidden tax" on self-pay patients, because health care providers receive only cents on the dollar from Medicare and Medicaid for their services. They also have negotiated fees with insurance plans. That leaves providers with the need to make up the difference somewhere, often from self-pay or cash-only patients.

Samaritan also educates members on how to seek discounts from providers themselves, before they even submit bills to SMI. The ministry also makes services like Healthcare Bluebook and MediBid available, helping members to shop around for the best pricing.

## Firing Up the Allocation Engine

Once negotiations are nearly complete and approximate need amounts set, these amounts must be divvied up according to the shares available that month. Samaritan's Information Technology and Services department (ITS) handles that task with a software allocation engine that matches need amounts with shares. If there aren't enough shares to meet all needs, the allocation engine will suggest pushing an amount of larger, yet-to-be-negotiated needs to the following month.

Once Cameron determines the amount the ministry can manage that month, he approves the allocation of shares. When needs outstrip shares available in a given month—even with postponing some needs—prorating kicks in, meaning only a percentage of needs for that month are shared, typically settling around 80 to 85 percent. During times of prorating, members are urged to donate to a pro rata fund. Those with prorated needs can then apply to the fund for more money to meet their need. Some members send additional money directly to the assigned need. A suggested amount is included on the share slip.

Pro rata sharing doesn't go on for long, though. A frequent need to prorate indicates a trend of higher health care costs or some other cause that will need to be addressed. According to the Samaritan Guidelines, once three straight months of prorating occur, "members will be provided an opportunity to vote on whether they want to increase the monthly share."[18] Appropriate amounts are proposed and then voted on.

On the other side, if there are substantially more shares available than needs in a month, with no indication that the following month will see this trend reverse, members' assigned shares can actually be reduced.[19]

As the member with the need receives shares from other members, he or she uses a checklist to note assigned households that have sent their shares. Later in the month, the members send the checklist to Samaritan. When a member doesn't receive a share, Member Services contacts the member who failed to send the share to check on that household's circumstances. If financial problems are interfering with the ability of a household to send its shares, the ministry tries to help resolve the problem. Sometimes this can be handled through its sponsorship program, which temporarily helps families in tough financial situations. Eventually, though, a share may be reassigned to another member.

# SHARING THE BURDEN

As an early Samaritan staffer, Jason Morris followed up on shares that hadn't been sent. He grasped how important it was for members to receive the checks others were assigned to send them.

"If someone didn't send a $120 check (which was the family-level share amount at the time), that was a problem for somebody else," Morris said. "I felt a heavy burden of making sure those checks got to where they were supposed to be going. It became a life mission for me to track those things down and make sure those people understood there was somebody on the other end who didn't get their full need met."

A member's inability to send a share is a rare event, though. As the Bible's prescribed means of meeting each other's needs, health care sharing is also wise stewardship. As such, it is usually less expensive than health insurance, and more fulfilling.

# 11

# THE STORIES

One of the advantages of being a Samaritan Ministries member is hearing stories of healing and provision from God. They're printed in the monthly Newsletter and the Prayer Guide as well as published online.

## Tracy and Jeffrey Kamprath

Tracy and Jeffrey Kamprath, who faced the daunting situation of Tracy's brain cancer described in chapter 1, joined Samaritan in 2004. They stayed with the ministry even after Jeffrey changed jobs and his new employer offered insurance benefits. The Kampraths stuck with Samaritan because their monthly share was less expensive than Jeffrey's portion of an insurance premium would have been. They also liked the idea of sending shares from home to home rather than through a third party, meaning they knew where their money was going.

Yet it wasn't until after Tracy's treatment for the brain tumor that the Kampraths were "100 percent" sold on Samaritan.

"I wouldn't trade it for anything," Tracy said. "It was far easier to me than any insurance system that I've ever dealt with."

Whenever Tracy talked to Member Services Specialist Jeremy Beach, she always experienced "kindness, patience, and trust."

"That trust was really important," Tracy said. "It makes me want to be that much more careful and just trust that what I'm writing down is truthful and honest, and I think it's a beautiful image of the Body of Christ and how we work together."

## Bob and Kelly Rutan

Bob and Kelly Rutan have found that being part of Samaritan doesn't just save them money for health care; it also makes them more responsible for managing their own health. They are able to seek medical help from the provider they choose while avoiding unnecessary tests and expensive procedures. That helps them steward their (and Samaritan members') money. They also make fewer doctor appointments than they did in the past.

"We don't need to, praise the Lord," Kelly said. "We put our money into our health, and we don't buy lots of new clothes. We put our money into quality food, since that's the fuel for our bodies. We go to chiropractors and do wellness and herbal remedies. By treating ourselves with herbs, we don't have to get a lot of pharmaceuticals; we don't have to have a lot of doctors' visits. We try not to engage in behaviors that are going to cost you [other members] medical bills."

That is another of Samaritan's benefits, said Special Counsel Ray King. Members know that if they overuse the ministry by sharing ever-increasing bills, the monthly share amounts will go up—in the same way overuse of health insurance causes premiums to rise. By taking responsibility for how they spend dollars on health care, Samaritan and other HCSM members help to keep share amounts down. Responsible health practices have a direct impact on their financial situation.

The ministry's impact on the Rutan family doesn't stop with their physical health and their checkbook. It's spiritual as well.

When they are having family devotions and open up a prayer guide to read of a need they can pray for, "it takes us beyond the walls of our home."

"When our children read through the prayer guide, they have a very sympathetic heart for people and want to pray for them, also realizing that God has been gracious to us," Kelly said.

## The Moore family

Jay and Lori Moore of Bozeman, Montana, also felt God's grace after they joined Samaritan in 2007. The owners of a snowboard and skateboard business, the Moores had been members of Medi-Share until that year, but the state of Montana decided that sharing plan too closely resembled insurance. The family started searching for options, which led them to Samaritan. When they saw a newsletter piece on the National Association of Nouthetic Counselors (now the Association of Certified Biblical Counselors, or ACBC), they felt even more drawn to Samaritan. Lori and Jay were working toward ACBC certification as Biblical counselors.

In mid-2008, a lump developed on the neck of their then-15-year-old son, Collin. It was on the left side, right below his chin, said Jay. A doctor identified the lump as a swollen lymph node and assured them they had nothing to worry about. But the lump grew. Finally, the physician decided he needed to examine it more closely. When Collin came down with tonsillitis, the doctor decided to remove the offending lymph node. He told Jay and Lori that if the node were cancerous, he wouldn't take out both the tonsils and the lymph node—just the tonsils. The node turned out to be cancerous.

A biopsy identified the growth as a large B-cell lymphoma. That was good news, since that type of lymphoma is "way more treatable" than the more aggressive rhabdomyosarcoma, which doctors had told the Moores they might find. That meant Collin could be treated in Bozeman and live at home instead of having to stay at a children's hospital in Portland, Oregon, for six months for the more serious kind. Collin fought through the chemotherapy treatments, suffering the customary nausea, hair loss, and fatigue, but no other serious side effects.

Just as Collin started chemo treatments, the first part of the family's need appeared in the newsletter. "Checks started arriving," Jay said, "and kept coming."

"I was kind of surprised that 95 to 98 percent of the people who were supposed to be sending gifts *did*," Jay said.

Some members who weren't able to send shares in their assigned month eventually caught up.

"Every day, the mail would come, and three or four more checks would be in there," Jay said. "My son would go to sleep, and my daughter and I would sit at the kitchen table and read through the letters. She would call out check numbers and help me do a deposit slip. We'd wait until that deposit slip was filled up and then go and make a deposit in our account."

Jay's only regret: They hadn't joined Save to Share. He figured that since the Moores had a healthy family, their needs wouldn't exceed the then-standard ministry cap of $100,000. The original total of the bills came to $190,000. The Karis Group negotiated that down to about $160,000, leaving the Moores with $60,000 of expenses. A gift from a private donor and some fundraising efforts—an auction, a church charity event, and a niece who shaved people's heads bald for a contribution—reduced that amount to about $25,000. That still represented a steep obligation for the family. (Needless to say, the Moores quickly joined Save to Share, which they advise all members to do.)

Maneuvering their way through these challenges meant they especially appreciated the help they received from Doug Chamberlain, the Member Services specialist they worked with most closely. Though now in remission, at the time, Doug himself was undergoing treatment for lymphoma.

"It was really interesting to be able to call him up and say, 'Hey, we're praying for ya,' and hear him say, 'We're praying for Collin,'" Jay recalled. "Knowing that people really were praying for each other was huge."

Those prayers were answered, apparently for God's purposes. Later Jay reported that "Collin is doing well, seemingly completely healthy." Blood work came back clear: "Praise God," Jay said. Collin hopes to eventually become a missionary bush pilot.

## Ron and Debbie Walker

The news wasn't as good for Ron Walker, though.

He and his wife, Debbie, joined Samaritan early in 2009. The healthy Texas couple had never had health insurance. Both were self-employed. Ron operated a horse-drawn carriage business and did some meat-cutting on the side, while Debbie worked as a licensed massage therapist. Then Ron "felt in [his] spirit" that he should start looking around for some way to take care of health care needs. Underwhelmed by the "insurance the world has to offer," a neighbor suggested he call Samaritan Ministries.

"I didn't know what it was," he said, but after he found out more, it resonated with Debbie and him.

"What I liked about Samaritan Ministries was the idea of sending a note to someone who has a need versus just sending the money to a main office and they pay everything," Ron said. "It kind of leaves you out. In Samaritan, you actually put your faith in practice."

As "praying people," the emphasis on regularly petitioning the Lord for others' needs also appealed to the Walkers.

They soon needed those prayers. A little more than two months after joining Samaritan, a doctor diagnosed Debbie with a brain tumor. During her initial treatments, the Walkers racked up nearly $200,000 in medical bills. Negotiations and hospital write-offs brought that amount down to about $53,000, which was shared by Samaritan members.

"Good Shepherd Hospitals were wonderful to work with," Ron said. "It's something you don't want someone to go through and have to learn about, but when you do it, it's a learning experience. It helps you know how to pray for other members. Your guys [at Samaritan] have been very understanding and helpful."

Sadly, but in God's perfect will, Debbie's cancer attacked again in spring 2010. She died on September 27, 2010, after 34 years of marriage.

## Vincent and Maria

Maria, a 72-year-old native Italian, also remains with Samaritan years after the death of her husband, Vincent. His fatal illness left her facing a "mountain of hospital bills."

Vincent and Maria originally lived in the Italian village of Madeira but moved to England in 1963 when Vincent found a good job there. After their children grew up and moved to the US, Vincent and Maria followed.

"What do you do when you are old?" Maria said. "You move to be close to your children."

As new immigrants who had not worked in the US, the couple was not eligible for Medicare. For a while they managed to cope without health care assistance. Relatively healthy, Vincent and Maria paid cash the few times they had to visit a doctor.

One Sunday at church, though, they heard about Samaritan Ministries from a visiting pastor. Maria's son and her husband began investigating health care sharing. They were especially intrigued, because England, with its national health care system, didn't have anything like it. At first, Vincent and Maria wondered if they would be accepted due to their age; at the time of joining, Vincent was 73, Maria 66. But since age isn't a factor in qualifying for Samaritan membership, SMI welcomed them to the ministry in February 2009.

Only a few months later, Vincent had chest pains and went into the hospital for triple-bypass heart surgery. Four days later, he suffered a massive stroke that left him paralyzed and unable to see or speak. After five weeks, he passed away.

As Maria grieved the loss of her beloved husband, a second shock struck when she learned his hospital bills alone totaled $244,000. Doctors' bills would add to the stack. She and her daughter-in-law, Amy, met with hospital officials, telling them Maria couldn't pay it even if she sold her house.

"By God's grace, they discounted it all," Maria said. "That was a miracle."

However, they still had to take care of the doctors' bills.

"This is where Samaritan came in," Maria said. "My daughter-in-law phoned each doctor. They all gave discounts, except the radiologists."

The need arising from those bills came to $18,000. Maria waited to see whether Samaritan Ministries, which she had joined only a few months before, would come to her aid. Many times, she thought, "Is this really true? Will I receive the shares that will help me with this great need?"

After the need was published, Maria got her answer when the first check from another member arrived in the mail.

"I just sat there with that check in my hand, and I cried," she said. "It was hard to take in. I was truly overwhelmed and asked God to forgive me for my lack of trust. One by one, the shares kept coming, and the need [was] met."

Maria said the experience was "a great lesson in trust for me, and I really think this is the way that God intended it to be for His children, helping one another in our time of need. Each and every gift had a note in it. It was such a comfort to read them. Now [that] I know this way is true, I look forward to sending my monthly share for the needs of others."

As for signing up for Medicare, Maria still isn't sure if she's eligible.

"I never checked," she said. "I'm content with Samaritan."

## Trevor and Aimee Tindle

Trevor and Aimee Tindle of Oklahoma faced several challenges after the birth of their third child, Matthew, in 2012.

One was Matthew's health. His low blood sugar led doctors to put him in the neonatal intensive care unit (NICU). Once in the NICU, his blood sugar normalized. However, when he developed an infection, a doctor put him on antibiotics for 10 days, extending his stay in the unit.

The other challenges were financial and spiritual. The Tindles had left health insurance behind in 2011 to join Samaritan

Ministries. Their first need with the ministry came with Aimee's pregnancy the following year. Despite the steep costs of Matthew's delivery and subsequent treatment, all went well.

"It was easy," she said. "I told the front office lady at the doctor's that we would be private pay. Her exact words were, 'Oh, thank goodness.' She was so happy that they didn't have to deal with insurance. I was like, 'Great; works for you, works for me.'"

Aimee's obstetrician gave her a printout of his fees. Samaritan members shared those expenses prior to Matthew's birth, a unique feature of the ministry's sharing process—and an example of how much the ministry values human life.

As Aimee and Trevor waited for Matthew's antibiotics treatment to run its course, the financial reality of 10 days in the NICU became apparent.

"I thought, 'This is going to be a pretty big need,'" Aimee said. Still, it didn't scare them.

"We had such a peace about it," she said. "We were totally focused on Matthew. We didn't have to worry about it. We knew the bills were going to be large. But we had such a peace about being with Samaritan at that point. We called and you guys prayed with us. It just put us at ease, that, 'Hey, let's pray for the baby, and we'll deal with the other stuff whenever it comes.' It really was amazing."

The hospital didn't have such a peace about it. Once they discovered Trevor and Aimee didn't have health insurance, they sent a social worker to them, trying to get them to sign up for government assistance.

"We were like, 'No, listen, this is something that we really, truly believe God is going to provide,'" Aimee said.

One of the social workers Aimee talked to told her that she wasn't sure "the little ministry you're a part of is going to be able to handle this large NICU bill," which at that point was $20,000.

"That kind of tested me a little bit," Aimee said. "But I immediately said, 'No, we believe the Lord will provide through the members of this ministry.'"

And He did.

"It really did go very smoothly, the whole process. I was really amazed," Aimee said. "We had a wad of checks coming in."

They kept track of the 110 checks from other members, checked the payments off their list, deposited the funds in the bank, and paid their bills.

"I still have every card and letter that came, in a box," Aimee said. "It's just amazing to look back and think, 'Wow, all of those people were praying for my baby who was sick.'

"I wish I could put into words how I feel about the ministry, because it has been such a blessing. If something happens, I know that I'm going to have a lot of people praying. I know that God uses this ministry to take care of His people."

Just as He took care of Matthew, who, seven years later, is doing just fine.

# 12

# SMI IS FAMILY

Samaritan Ministries is a family inside and out. This ethic reflects the origins of the ministry, right down to Ted and Shari Pittenger and their children assembling the first Samaritan mailings at the dining room table in their Washington, Illinois, home.

The family atmosphere extends from the ministry's headquarters to its members. This happens through the SMI newsletter, prayer team, prayer guide, internet communications, Member Services teams, staff gatherings, and "stuffing day." That last of these derived its name from the monthly bundling of newsletter and share-slip information for mailing. This joyous occasion was often accompanied by the sound of children's laughter and running feet echoing down the hallway. If you stopped in on one of those days, you were liable to hear Samaritan Executive Vice President James Lansberry say something rarely, if ever, heard at the office of a successful enterprise: "Just try not to put your fingers on the wall, okay?"

Bryan Evans, former vice president of Member Services, said the family emphasis was "one of the first things that jumped out at me" when he joined the ministry. Not too long after he started, membership had grown enough that newsletter stuffing couldn't be accomplished solely by staff. The biggest pool of volunteer workers comprised staff members' spouses and children. They started coming in once a month to collate newsletter materials while Samaritan employees handled the share slips. That practice continued even as membership topped 30,000 households in early 2014. The newsletter went out on time, thanks to the family members who augmented staffers' efforts.[20]

One of Samaritan's strengths, according to Bryan, is allowing employees' spouses and children to volunteer at the ministry, thus allowing a family to labor together for the Lord. Samaritan wants its staff to be involved in family life, instead of sucking the energy out of a worker and damaging the person's family in the process. Except in unusual circumstances, staff aren't expected to work more than 40 hours a week.

"I can't imagine an employee-employer relationship more family-friendly than ours," Bryan said.

As Samaritan membership and staff have grown, creating a need for larger buildings, maintaining the original "community feel" has posed a challenge. In the past, the entire ministry staff assembled for coffee and pastries on an employee's last day, but only departments do that now—although Human Resources Director Justin Easley still refers to departments as "family units."

"Lord willing, we don't get to the day that you could walk around the offices and not recognize many of the staff," DeWayne Arington said.

Such a scenario was unlikely during the early days at the chicken coop and little house, when fewer than a dozen employees composed the SMI staff. Even in the Marquette Heights building, with most of the employees working in the large, open sanctuary, community came easy—especially with acoustics that carried conversations from one side to the other and even to Ted's office down the hall.

The coziness did lead to the occasional need to shut things off for some individuals, leading to a "culture of headphones," Seth Ben-Ezra said. "You were trying to close off a little bit of the world and get some privacy.

"If you really wanted to escape, you went back to the Subscription Development (now Member Development) office, which in time became known as 'South Dakota,'" he continued. "You had one primary working area where most of the people were. You could hear each other. And then you had the one primary hangout. That was where the chessboard was. South Dakota was the cool department. You could hang out there and get out of the way, as long as you weren't too rowdy when somebody was actually on the phone with an inquirer. You could talk with Bryan Evans or Anthony Hopp."

Spicing things up, many of the devoted Christians at Samaritan were willing to debate pretty much any topic, especially theological subjects. For relief from what Bryan Evans called the "insane amount of work," there were practical jokes, singing, and general silliness. When it was someone's birthday, everyone would jump into Bryan's 15-passenger van and go out to lunch.

"It was a tight-knit, family culture," Bryan said.

Reflecting this laid-back atmosphere, things weren't organized in a highly structured manner. Staff members generally did whatever was needed if the need arose (and if they were capable). Now responsibilities are clearly delineated, with a Systems department that has merged with Information Technology to help departments work more smoothly together.

## Business and Ministry

Samaritan faces a challenge that any ministry does: having one foot in business and one in ministry—and trying to do both well.

"We're fully committed to being a ministry, but also fully committed to being run properly, as a business would be," said Bryan Evans.

With challenges increasing amid ministry growth, leaders recognized some key lessons:

- Those who are in charge need to grow with the organization. "Just because someone is competent to do a certain job at size X doesn't mean that person is competent to do the same job at size 2X," James Lansberry said. "In order to serve the members well, we have to make sure people are in the right places and that we are hiring the right people to balance for weaknesses."

- Training is needed at all levels. Executive VP James Lansberry and Human Resources VP Justin Easley have each earned an Executive Master of Business Administration degree at Peoria's Bradley University. "Not that I have a yearning to have letters after my name," James said. "I knew there was a need to either find someone else who can do my job better than me, or have *me* be the person who can do my job better than me."

- Running a larger organization requires additional skills. Both staff and membership have tripled in size in the past few years. Samaritan is managing more money and people. "All of that takes different ideas of which practices will work at 10,000 members and which practices will work at 70,000 members," Lansberry said. "Operating principles are not the same."

- Employees who used to divide their time between tasks now find themselves focusing on single areas of expertise. Lansberry said that is a matter of reliability, especially as needs in technology—such as 24/7 internet access—expand.

- As the ministry has grown, SMI has needed to put disaster recovery plans and other crisis-management plans in place.

The move to a larger facility in 2005 presented other challenges to a family-style culture. Suddenly workers were spread out in different rooms, offices, and cubicles. Despite a common kitchen and dining room, people ate lunch on varying schedules. This necessitated intentional efforts to maintain a community atmosphere, such as a monthly luncheon where all staff members gathered. After the meal, they heard ministry updates and a leader's teaching from Scripture. Those gatherings have been adjusted as the staff has grown and a second facility has been added, but there's still a monthly staff meeting at a local church, monthly lunches provided at the two buildings, and monthly or weekly department meetings.

Some of the meetings include a time of worship—no problem with SMI's plethora of musicians and singers.

The weekly staff prayer time, initiated during the health care reform push in Washington, DC, continues today. After seeing God answer those prayers in the form of an exemption from the health insurance mandate, organizers felt led to make this an ongoing feature. The Tuesday morning prayer time was another way to keep staffers apprised of each other's needs, members' needs, and the ministry's needs. The ministry's growth led to scheduling a second session, with weekly prayer times now on Wednesday and Friday mornings.

Staff members also have an annual opportunity to meet with the Samaritan Board of Directors. January Board meetings are typically held at Samaritan headquarters in Peoria. Members who arrive early usually set aside time for one-on-one meetings with ministry employees, an opportunity unique to ministries like Samaritan.

"How many mailroom employees at major corporations get the opportunity to meet with Board members?" asked Justin Easley.

Managers also ask employees to anonymously complete the Best Christian Workplaces Survey each year. The results have been good, with Samaritan being voted a "Best Christian Workplace" for 11 consecutive years. Suggestion boxes are posted in both buildings, and leadership answers questions at monthly staff-wide meetings.

Friendships extend across levels of authority. Instead of blurring professional boundaries, these friendships facilitate authentic exchanges.

"Because we're first Christians, if we go by Matthew 18, it takes some of the risk away to be friends," Justin said. "When we are friends, it's easier to be honest."

In fact, Justin said, even a "higher-up" like Lansberry has asked Justin to keep him accountable. And when the ministry has a need, it's "all hands on deck." Staffers from all departments, including officers, helped prepare mailings on stuffing day.

"It's all going to come back to what's best for the members," Justin said. "This ministry exists to honor God. It's just that we're doing that through health care."

## Hiring for the Culture

Samaritan's healthy work atmosphere is partly due to smart hiring priorities. Justin said the ministry makes hiring decisions based more on character than talent—and how well the individual will fit into SMI's culture. Leaders reason that, because skills can be learned, it makes more sense to hire people with good character who can grow into their position.

"I don't know if a person's an awesome software developer, but I *do* know what it will take to be an awesome cultural fit here," Justin said. "Chemistry is a really big thing. If a person is an IT development whiz but a social jerk, we're not bringing him on. You have to have the ability to do the work as well, though."

Samaritan has been blessed in recent years with the addition of former pastors and chaplains to its Member Services advocate team. Their experience in ministry helps them as they assist members with health care and personal issues.

That emphasis on character rather than on business savvy helps the ministry—even as it grows—to retain its informal feel. That reflects the desire of Founder Ted Pittenger, who recalled visiting the office of a bartering group in Chicago while still operating his painting business.

"This guy comes walking in, and he's got blue jeans, a work shirt, and cowboy boots on," Ted said. "He walked in like he knew what he was doing."

He did. Ted found out he was the owner.

"I thought, 'That's what I want to be when I grow up,'" Ted recalled. "'I want to go to work in blue jeans, a work shirt, and cowboy boots.'"

As he recounted the incident during a normal workday at Samaritan, Ted wore jeans, a Hawaiian shirt instead of a work shirt, and tennis shoes instead of cowboy boots. Most importantly, "None of this tie stuff."

"I've been on both sides of that," he said. "I went through a time in college where I didn't wear blue jeans for a whole year.

I just got in my mind, 'I'm a child of the King, I should dress specially,' so I did that."

However, thanks to a natural tendency toward casual dress, this became the unofficial dress code at the office. Casual, but not sloppy, is the guideline. No T-shirts or shorts.[21] The rumor circulates that at Samaritan Ministries, two things will get you fired right away: failure to recycle aluminum cans, and wearing a tie. The latter stems from Ted's relaxed attitude. The former comes from his belief in being good stewards of the earth, which God placed under man's dominion.

"If I wasn't a Christian, I'd probably be some environmental wacko or something," Ted said. "I have a theory you could get to zero garbage if you recycled everything and had a compost pile."

His wife sometimes teases Ted about his relaxed demeanor.

"He'll go to the hardware store in his grubby stuff because he's been working at home, and I'll say, 'Wow, you don't look like the President of Samaritan Ministries,'" Shari said. "He says, 'Yeah, that's okay.'"

## Difficult to Leave

This laid-back, tight-knit work atmosphere makes it hard for people to leave.

"They made it a place where you want to work," said Jason Morris, who departed in February 2008 for a time after a decade with the ministry but is now back as Director of Member Experience and Strategic Relationships. "The Samaritan job wasn't like other jobs. There was a sense of family there. You knew that if something went wrong at your house, DeWayne Arington would show up and fix it."

When the three-year-old daughter of another Samaritan staffer passed away, the question wasn't how soon he could get back to work, but how much time he needed. His supervisor made sure he knew he could leave on a moment's notice if needed at home, without worrying about whether it counted as personal time.

"The heart of the people here, they're family, man," Jason said. "We grew together. We grew up together in a lot of ways."

Andy Tharp didn't want to leave Samaritan, either. However, after four years at the Peoria ministry, in 2006 he and his wife felt God calling them to minister at a church in Georgia. Andy kept a foot in the ministry by negotiating bill reductions for members in Georgia, North Carolina, and Tennessee. He still works with Samaritan members by serving with The Karis Group.

Still, Tharp acknowledged the difficulties of leaving SMI behind.

"I was able to get up every day and go to work and help people, pray for them, pray with them, and help their bills get shared and their bills get paid," Andy recalled. "It was the only job I had where I didn't stress about getting up and going to work."

## Expanding Horizons

Working at Samaritan isn't only a "less-stress" career. It helps employees relate more easily to other members of the Body of Christ. One advantage to working at a multidenominational ministry like Samaritan is having positive interactions with Christians despite differing theological doctrines. Samaritan staffers come from Presbyterian, Baptist, nondenominational evangelical, Reformed, Pentecostal, Lutheran, and even messianic Jewish backgrounds. Others have an Apostolic Christian or Mennonite heritage.

Yet, Bryan said, this isn't a "check your brain at the door" form of ecumenism. Heated theological discussions still occasionally erupt in the hallway, lunchroom, or a meeting—yet maintain the quality of respect.

Andy Tharp counted himself among those able to shed long-held prejudices against other denominations because of working at Samaritan.

"I was raised as a Baptist," he said. "Baptists are pretty strict in a lot of ways. Some look down on other denominations. At Samaritan, I was surrounded by several different denominations of churches. I quickly learned that these people are genuinely true Christians. Some of them are a ton better than I am when it comes to Christianity. It was a true spiritual experience working at Samaritan. I thought it was neat that God would bring us all together and we could get along and accomplish something."

Morris called it one of the ministry's strengths. Jason grew up Lutheran and later started attending an Assemblies of God church, which led him to be more open to spiritual gifts. He thought about that when Ted interviewed him, and they got involved in a discussion about speaking in tongues.

"I've never spoken in tongues, but I'm not closed to it," Ted told Jason.

"When Ted said that, it was kind of the antithesis of everything I had heard in the church world," Jason remembered years later. "If you have a leader like Ted, you can virtually guarantee you're going to have a ministry that's not going to lean one way."

Or, as Psalm 133:1 puts it: "Behold, how good and pleasant it is when brothers dwell in unity!"

# 13

# SMI IS A BIG FAMILY

Samaritan is nothing, of course, without its larger family: the members. They are the ones who share each other's health care burdens, who pray for healing and comfort for each other, and who encourage one another.

In the early days, they were called "subscribers," which helped set the ministry apart from insurance. With the monthly *Christian Health Care Newsletter*, which members subscribed to, came a share slip containing the name and address of the person whose need they were assigned to share that month, and a note of how to pray for that person. The term "subscription" eventually gave way to "membership," yet the concept remained the same.

Whether called *subscribers* or *members*, the people who join Samaritan make up one part of the Body of Christ. They enable other parts of that Body to strengthen and help one another carry their burdens in times of need. Samaritan leaders have sought to maintain this sense of family, demonstrating practical, charitable Christianity in action.

"It's a way we can care for one another, in a real way, and not just say, 'Be warm, be filled,'" said Executive Vice President James Lansberry, referring to the practical action called for in James 2:15-16.

Genuine caring is even reflected in Samaritan's legendary Groundhog database. The default search mode is for members' names, not a number. Account numbers can be helpful internally when dealing with more than 82,000 active member households and thousands of former member households. "But we try to make sure as we're dealing with them that we call them by name and ask them how they prefer to be addressed," Lansberry said.

All of this relates to Samaritan's emphasis on the continual teaching in Scripture of caring for "one another." As Lansberry says, "Samaritan facilitates community on a large scale, and facilitates people caring for one another."

This is emphasized at all levels: Full-time Samaritan employees are required to maintain SMI membership. This helps them understand exactly what non-employee members experience and deal with month to month, as well as to identify with the bigger "family" they serve.

## Power of Prayer

The shares sent by members to other members are helpful, but with Samaritan Ministries, the Lord may be working more directly through prayer than through the US Postal Service.

"In pretty much all communications with members, we will ask them to pray," said Special Counsel Ray King, "If we want the right things to happen, they aren't going to happen unless we pray. Some people would say, 'All you're going to do is *pray*?' If we have a fund-raiser, we say, 'If you can't give, please pray.' We think when people pray, God will answer those prayers. Sometimes, prayers are answered before we ever know we need the answer."

Ray tells the story of a Samaritan couple in Alaska who experienced the power of prayer. The wife lay in a hospital with a condition doctors couldn't diagnose. "All they knew was that she was deathly ill and not getting any better," Ray said. "They didn't know what to do."

The husband wrote that on the morning of his wife's scheduled transfer by life flight to another hospital, he entered her room to find her condition improving—and she continued to improve throughout the day. By the end of the afternoon, the doctor told the man that there was no reason to keep her there any longer.

When the couple got home, they opened their monthly newsletter from Samaritan, including the Prayer Guide. They discovered that the woman's name had been assigned for prayer . . . *on that day*. Members on the East Coast (several hours ahead of Alaska time), who prayed in the morning, had started the wave. Then it spread west across the United States and correlated with the improvement in the woman's condition.

Ironically, the odds of the Alaska members receiving the Prayer Guide with their request in it were pretty slim, since at that time approximately 20 different versions went into the mail. "And so the fact that they would receive one that had their request in it, so they would even be able to tell us that it had happened was kind of a sign that God's hand was there," Ray said. "Prayer is worth doing. It's worth keeping prayer at the forefront of everything we do."

Such stories are a primary reason prayer has long been featured in Samaritan's *Christian Health Care Newsletter*.

"We thought of the newsletter as a way to build a sense of community where we have some shared values, where you take people who are looking for a way to save money, but also people who are convinced this is a Biblical way to share needs,"

Ray said. "We have Member Spotlights that tell about members who have interesting ministries or accomplishments. We had the Final Rewards feature to honor those brothers and sisters who have gone on to their Final Reward."

Prayer requests were originally part of the newsletter itself, but as membership increased, the requests began to overwhelm the publication. Then Ray heard a seminar speaker who said that Christians would generally pray for one specific thing a day from a list broken down by day. After that, Ray changed how prayer needs were distributed. Instead of listing them in batch form and asking all members to pray for each, Samaritan started breaking them down to one per day, listed alphabetically, and printing as many versions of the Prayer Guide as needed to include all the needs. This practice continues, providing another tool to keep members connected without overwhelming them.

Requests in the Prayer Guide come from Member Services. When processing a need, member advocates include information in the database entry on how the need can be prayed for: member name, the problem, and whether it's an upcoming procedure, ongoing situation, or completed need.

The most direct prayer connection through Samaritan may be the monthly share notification, which tells a member where to send his or her monthly share. As in the case of the Alaskan couple, members are urged to pray for the person whose needs they are sharing that particular month. They are also urged to send an encouraging note along with their share (remembering the motto of "Send a note, pay your share, always stay alert in prayer"). Those notes and cards end up being quite meaningful.

"The cards and notes from others were such a blessing to us," a member named Darlene said in a note to Samaritan. "It definitely motivates us to give on time, pray, encourage someone else, and give extra when we can."

Members routinely mention the blessings of being part of Samaritan in their letters to the ministry. A few excerpts:

- "We have been so blessed to be a part of this ministry. Even when our need was prorated, God blessed us by causing the doctors and hospital to reduce their bill by that exact amount so that our need was met. Receiving the encouraging notes from our Christian brothers and sisters has always been the kindness and love that is needed. God's timing is great."—P.H., California

- "Single parenting is lonely, especially when dealing with a serious problem involving one of my children. I feel a sense of support from Samaritan Ministries. Thank you so much for what you do. There is no way to express the depth of my gratitude."—L.L.R., Texas

- "We are so grateful for the prayer support from everyone. We've had an ongoing need with cancer. We have saved all our cards and notes of encouragement. When we get tired or a little discouraged, we can look at our overflowing basket and pick one up and be blessed all over again."—D.H., Michigan

- "I am overwhelmed with God's goodness to His children. I never doubted that my larger bill would be reduced more than the original 15 percent, but when the hospital gave me a 91.5 percent discount, I was in awe of God's compassion to me. I am so very happy and pleased that there was almost $2,000 to send on to someone else within SMI for a medical emergency. It gave me peace and joy to belong to Samaritan Ministries."—J.I., Washington state

- "We are thankful to the Lord that we are a part of this ministry. Many times we have been asked to purchase insurance. When we respond that we are members of Samaritan Ministries and explain how it works, the insurance representatives always acknowledge that they cannot even come close to competing with that."—F.M., North Carolina

- "When my husband took the stacks of checks to the hospital to pay my bill, the receptionist was amazed. She called coworkers to come see for themselves. She said that it had revived her faith in humanity. People still do care about helping each other. Then she began to cry. Samaritan Ministries is truly a testimony of God's love for His children."—V. & D.E., Wisconsin

For Barb Lange, now Project Coordinator for the Creative Team, the opportunity to review this kind of correspondence was the most gratifying part of her job.

"It's within these letters that I truly see how God uses this ministry and His people," she said. "Countless times I've read accounts of people entering into the phase of having a need published and admit to being nervous about it by saying to themselves, 'Is this really going to work?' only to confess that not only did it work, but it worked beyond their expectations. Some of the most common responses are, 'It increased my faith,' or, 'I could feel the prayers of the saints,' or 'The letters came just when I needed them the most.' They follow up with comments like, 'When was the last time your insurance company wrote and told you they were praying for you, or you felt compelled to write your insurance company to say thank you?'

"More importantly, member letters are an opportunity for members to express their humble appreciation to and for a God who has taken them through the birth of their children or through many dark hours of sickness, loss, and pain."

All this prayer and encouragement occurs within a membership that is anything but uniform. The diversity of the ministry's membership is a testament to Samaritan's character as a work of God. The representation of Christian denominations and traditions among Samaritan members cuts a wide swath, reflecting the headquarters' staff. As long as a person can sign the basic statement of faith required for membership, have his or her Biblical lifestyle verified by church leadership, regularly send shares, and faithfully attend church, he or she qualifies as a member.

A unifying miracle takes place without many members even realizing it, drawing together Christians who would be hard-pressed to do one or more of the following:

- Sit in the same church together
- Sing the same worship songs
- Pray the same prayers in the same way
- Agree on many tangential matters of the faith

Samaritan members who diverge from each other on such matters somehow gladly send money to each other every month and—most importantly—pray for each other.

"We're meeting a need by helping them feel some security in that they've got the Body of Christ with them," Samaritan General Counsel Brian Heller said. "There's a human and brother-to-brother connection."

## Zeroing in on Unity

The ability to find that common Christian denominator is what creates the larger family aspect of Samaritan Ministries and contributes to its ever-expanding ability to continue sharing health care needs.

"What I see SMI doing as a service for our members is quite simple," Barb said. "We help them get in contact with like-minded people who desire to help with the financial burden of medical care, all the while introducing them to the side of God they may not be quite so familiar with . . . the intimate, passionate side of Jesus Christ."

That is by design. Ted Pittenger said that when he started Samaritan, he wanted to make sure a variety of Christians would be comfortable enough with its theological principles to join. On a mission trip to Europe with Shari and their daughter, Meg, in the summer of 1981, Ted heard a pastor say that doctrine is like a target with concentric circles. If you don't believe in a few fundamentals of the faith, you're outside even the outermost circle. But the more you agree with different aspects of the faith, the closer you move to the center. You might be off to the left or to the right, but you are still hitting the target.

That is how Samaritan's Statement of Faith has been used: to discern whether prospective members hit the target at all, let alone strike the center of the circle.

"We wanted to be as inclusive as possible," Ted said. "Our concept is that if you can sign off on this Statement of Faith, we can accept you. And maybe, as they read the newsletter, maybe that'll challenge them to think about their circumstances."

Diversity has even played itself out culturally among Samaritan members, Ted said. At one time, a member of a Christian heavy metal rock band was a Samaritan member. Ted contrasted him with another member known for being culturally conservative and opposing rock music.

"I thought, 'Here you've got two diverse members, and they can send money to each other, pray for and encourage each other, but they probably couldn't even sit down and eat a meal together,'" Ted said. "Now, that's pretty exciting, to think we're that bridge for people."

## 14

# WHERE WE ARE;
# WHERE WE'RE GOING

Samaritan Ministries remains at God's disposal. The ministry takes its stewardship and future obligations seriously, especially as it deals with the challenges and opportunities presented by continuing growth.

## A Bigger Building

Leadership has done its best to stay ahead of the growth curve. A prime example is Ted Pittenger's early 2010 forecast that the ministry would need a larger building to house additional employees to properly serve an ever-expanding group of members. Sensing the wisdom of such a move, leaders started reviewing new potential headquarter sites that year and ended up getting another "God-sent" deal.

Ted and the other officers looked at a couple of possibilities in nearby towns, but nothing seemed to fit SMI's needs or budget. Then the same realtor who had urged Samaritan leaders to "just make an offer" on its Altorfer Drive building contacted them after hearing of the ministry's plans. He told them of a listing of a larger building in Peoria next to a nature preserve. Ted looked up information about the site online; at $2.5 million, the listing was well above Samaritan's price range.

"The first time we went to look at the building, wild turkeys crossed in front of our car in the parking lot," Ted said. "It reminded me of our first purchased building in Marquette Heights. I felt like we were coming back home."

Again, the realtor said, "You need to make an offer."

While Samaritan had some cash reserves, Ted recalled how Board members were concerned that SMI might be "kind of presuming on God a little bit." However, after further reviewing the situation, they decided to revisit the possibilities.

"We basically said, 'All right, if the Lord brings in an additional $400,000 in the next 30 days, we'll have a clear sense that this is from Him,'" Ted said.

So, the directors approved a mailing to members informing them about the opportunity—and the need for more resources. The members responded with more than prayer. In three weeks, $300,000 in contributions flooded in to SMI's headquarters.

More money came from a well-timed bump in new memberships, with their initial membership fees bringing additional cash flow.

"The Lord definitely gave us an indication that we should move ahead," Ray King said.

"When we sat down and calculated it out, it was like, 'Hey, the Lord provided the money,'" Ted said. "How could we *not* move forward?"

Ultimately, in late 2010, Samaritan purchased the 57,000-square-foot building and its accompanying 12 acres for $1.6 million—$900,000 less than the original asking price. God had come through in more ways than one. Not only did the relocation take place several months later, but in another sign of God's hand over SMI, the ministry's Altorfer Drive building sold for $600,000. It did so in unusually quick fashion amid a stale real estate market—one still reeling from the 2008 housing collapse that sparked the Great Recession.

SMI projected that its "Forest Park" facility (next to the Forest Park Nature Center) would give it the capacity to house enough staffers to serve up to 50,000 member households. As the ministry quickly approached and surpassed that number in the wake of the Affordable Care Act, a second building—a former roller rink—located about a mile and a half away was purchased, giving Samaritan another 27,600 square feet to work with. It also has allowed staff to experiment with communications between separate locations.

## The Morning Center

Samaritan Ministries was never meant to be solely about health care sharing. The ministry's bylaws state that its purpose is to carry out the Great Commission given in Matthew 28:18-20:

> And Jesus came and said to them, "All authority in Heaven and on earth has been given to me. Go therefore and make disciples of all nations, baptizing them in the name of the Father and of the Son and of the Holy Spirit, teaching them to observe all that I have commanded you. And behold, I am with you always, to the end of the age."

A subpoint of those bylaws, however, states that carrying out that mission includes "developing and operating ministries that provide resources to facilitate and promote the ability of Christians throughout the Body of Christ to be obedient disciples." That includes health care sharing and educating members through the *Christian Health Care Newsletter*, but it also involves creating mechanisms to bless people in other ways.

A big step along those lines was taken in 2011 by James Lansberry and his wife, Theresa, which led to the formation of the Morning Center. For several years the Lansberrys had been drawn toward ministering to pregnant women in difficult circumstances after they learned that Medicaid paid for half of all childbirths in their previous home state of South Carolina. The couple believed that the Church could do better for these women and their babies.

"Medicaid pays for 41 percent of childbirths nationwide," James said. "It's time for Christians to take the beginning-of-life ministry back for Jesus's glory. We want to step in and give women an option of maternity care that takes into account the image of God in both the mother and the child. We want to offer an alternative to the second-class service most mothers currently receive through Medicaid."

Enter the Morning Center. "In contrast to Medicaid," James said, "the Morning Center offers high-quality, personalized, charitable maternity care from the start of a pregnancy through the sometimes difficult postpartum period for women and children who need it. Since human beings are created in God's image, the maternity and birth experience should be the best available rather than settling for the low-quality care that typically accompanies Medicaid's low reimbursement rates."

"God's image will be glorified instead of demeaned," Lansberry said.

James believed so deeply in the idea that—if necessary—he was prepared to leave Samaritan Ministries to launch this new ministry. He didn't need to, though. Ted Pittenger decided that a ministry like the Morning Center fit perfectly with Samaritan's mission. The SMI Board of Directors approved the project, and the development of the Morning Center initiated soon after the vote. It took its name from an existing project headed by Samaritan staffers Tom Candler and Micah Repke. The pair had started the original Morning Center project with the goal of creating a public memorial to aborted children. They envisioned collecting one cent for each child aborted in the United States since the fateful US Supreme Court ruling of 1973 opened the floodgates for this practice. As longtime pro-life activists, Candler and Repke gladly agreed to apply the name of their project to the Lansberrys' vision.

The original idea targeted the establishment of birthing centers in cities with the greatest need. However, regulatory reality soon intervened. Morning Center leaders discovered that laws friendly to existing hospitals required any new health care facilities to qualify for a "certificate of need." Ostensibly, these facilities had to prove the need for their services in a specific community, but, this requirement posed a formidable challenge: the health care environment politically favored existing facilities.

Instead of focusing on opening a permanent facility—at least during its start-up phase—the Morning Center hit the road, announcing plans in November 2011 to place mobile maternity units in three cities. Besides avoiding the regulatory and political entanglements of a permanent location, at $100,000 per unit, these mobile facilities were a fraction of the cost of a maternity hospital. It also allowed the ministry to serve needy women in their own communities and during unconventional hours.

The ministry selected three cities gauged to have strong support from the local pro-life community and the greatest need: Indianapolis, Indiana; Charlotte, North Carolina; and Memphis, Tennessee. The barometers for need included unemployment rates, infant mortality rates, the percentage of people living below federal poverty levels, and a need for increased medical services.

Memphis wound up as the first city to receive a facility providing pregnancy tests and ultrasounds. Morning Center personnel began seeing expectant mothers in the summer of 2013, and the first baby born to a client came into the world the following January. By early 2019, more than 570 babies had been born with Morning Center help.

Long-range plans still include a full-service maternity hospital, with all high-quality services provided free of charge. Another Morning Center is being started in Atlanta.

## Legislative Efforts

Samaritan also continues to focus on its original function: helping Christians to share each other's health care burdens. To do that, it has to stay in touch with legislators on the state and federal levels. The federal-level health care reform experience served as notice that "our public policy department is going to be around for a long time," James Lansberry said.

"Now that we're on the radar screen in Washington, DC, we need to continue to watch what's going on there," he continued. "There's no delusion on our part that this was a short-term race that's now over, and we can go back to 'business as usual.'"

Samaritan's Public Policy department has worked for safe-harbor laws for HCSMs on the state level, securing in law the right to operate in 30 states without being subjected to the same kind of requirements, such as financial reserves, applied to insurance companies.[22] Such laws remove ambiguity when states deal with health care sharing ministries, but with the Affordable Care Act requiring health care plans to be portable from state to state, James Lansberry says, "It's less important than before." Plus, six of the eight states with the largest number of Samaritan members—Florida, Illinois, Indiana, Pennsylvania, Texas, and

WHERE WE ARE; WHERE WE'RE GOING

Washington—have safe-harbor laws. Two-thirds of Samaritan members live in states with such safeguards.

The Alliance of Health Care Sharing Ministries and Samaritan's Public Policy department also have been working at the federal level for HCSM members to qualify for health savings accounts (HSAs) if they don't already have access to one. HSAs allow people to save money in tax-free accounts and use it for qualified medical expenses. These include such expenses as visits to a doctor's office, prescriptions, dental and vision needs, and other incidental costs that fall below Samaritan's $300/$1,500 thresholds (or don't fit within the Guidelines), depending on membership in Samaritan Classic or Basic.

Samaritan is also working to help members deal with the impact of the Affordable Care Act. While HCSM members are exempt from the individual mandate, they still have to deal with its effects, such as some doctors possibly deciding to see only patients with insurance. If members have a hard time finding medical practices that will take self-pay patients (e.g., HCSM members), "then that impacts our ability to serve," James Lansberry said. "We have to look for ways that we can get out in front of that issue and make relationships with self-pay practices so they are ready to receive our members."

Public policy staffers also need to remain aware of developments in health care public policy. While the individual exemption for HCSM members is firmly ensconced in 26 United States Code Section 5000a, (d)(2)(B) of the ACA, "what the government giveth, the government can taketh away," Lansberry pointed out.

"We have to be wise as serpents and innocent as doves," he said. "But we're still not sacrificing our desire to speak the truth. We will remain consistent in our proclamation of a Biblical worldview. It also sets us more to prayer. We realize more and more that there isn't anything we can build that someone else can't take away, if God's not pleased with us. So we're asking for God to continue as He has over the past decade or more, to go before us, to protect us. I think we can say that the God who protected us from the state government of Washington, and the God who protected us from the Affordable Care Act, is able to protect us from whatever comes before us. There needs to be a constant rehearing of the stories of God's blessings so we can have the faith to walk forward and trust in His future blessings, even if the situation looks dire."

## Surge of Service

Samaritan General Counsel Brian Heller believes that Samaritan's best survival strategy is "to minister faithfully to our members."

"God will bless our faithfulness, which He's done," Brian said. "Government officials will respect us if we're faithfully ministering to our members."

More Christians are also seeing the spiritual value in health care sharing ministries. As government encroaches more on citizens' lives, more believers may yearn for a tightly knit community comprising "people who will help you in a time of need," Bryan Evans said. That certainly appears to be true with the implementation of the Affordable Care Act.

After health insurance exchanges opened on October 1, 2013, and the year-end deadline to have some kind of acceptable health insurance approached, Samaritan and the other health care sharing ministries saw record membership increases. Christians who didn't want to be saddled with high insurance premiums and deductibles, who were losing their health insurance, or who finally needed to get some kind of coverage for medical expenses so they wouldn't be penalized, started inundating ministry phone lines. Anthony Hopp, who was head of Membership Development at the time, called it a "phone burst." Calls overwhelmed the five specialists available to take them. Former Board member Jamie Pyles, who now makes Samaritan presentations to ministries and other groups, volunteered to take extra calls. At its peak, the deluge ranged from 115 to 130 calls a day.

While membership growth had been above projections all year, with 500 or 600 new starts a month, the final three months of 2013 and the first month of 2014 saw astonishing increases. After 1,155 new members in December, that number more than doubled a month later to 2,781, pushing Samaritan past 30,000 member households and 100,000 individuals served. Such explosive growth continued through September 2019, with the membership increasing to more than 82,000 households and more than 270,000 individuals.

## Sharing the Burden

Samaritan can and should continue to serve as an example of a better way of providing for Christians' health care needs. John Graham, formerly of the Pacific Research Institute and now a Regional Director at the US Department of Health and Human Services, says Samaritan and the other HCSMs model the "value of voluntary association, the benefit of people with similar values who really have an impulse to care for their brothers and sisters on their own initiative."

"Many of the players in the health care system have been so caught up in the government system that they can't see beyond that," Graham said. "They invest a lot of time and resources in satisfying what the government needs and not what the patients need."

Samaritan members realize they are a "part of a community in which health care expenses are being shared, and everybody has a responsibility not only to take care of themselves, but also to take care of the community and to make sure that everybody is spending those health care dollars wisely," said Grace-Marie Turner of The Galen Institute. "That's crucially important. If the rest of the country operated on that same model, you wouldn't have a health care crisis."

In other words, "Samaritan gets it," Turner continued. "They're community. They're family. They are paying these bills."

> Thus, Samaritan continues doing what it has done best since 1994—carrying out the vision Ted Pittenger sensed while praying in his chicken coop.

Thus, Samaritan continues doing what it has done best since 1994—carrying out the vision Ted Pittenger sensed while praying in his chicken coop. "I don't know that I've noticed a lot of change in the ministry," early member Elizabeth Garcia said. "It seems to keep functioning the way it did from the very beginning. It seems to have just remained the same. It continues to minister to us and allow us to minister to other people."

With God's provision, it will continue giving the thousands of members a place to turn to when the unexpected happens. It will continue to be a safe harbor for health care needs where prayer is at the forefront, where trust in God is commonplace, and where the Word of God reigns.

"What impresses me most is Samaritan remains true to the vision they had at the very beginning," said James Reid, listed as the ninth member to join the ministry. "They have not wavered from the call that has been placed upon them. They have done it in a way that has not burdened members in a significant way."

This happens not by accident, but by commitment. And, by the grace of God, it won't stop.

"We will continue to try to provide a mechanism to help Christians share medical bills with one another," James Lansberry said. "That comes from our desire to get members to understand their responsibility to each other as part of the Christian community."

And it will be done the way Ted and Shari Pittenger first envisioned it more than two decades ago, by Christians sending a note, paying their share, and always staying alert in prayer.

# ENDNOTES

## Chapter 1

1. The limit per need for those not in Samaritan's Save to Share™ (see chapter 6) has been $250,000 since July 2010.

2. Abby Goodnough, "Christians Flock to Groups That Help Members Pay Medical Bills," New York Times, March 10, 2016, 1.

3. 26 US Code 5000(a) and (d)(2)(b).

4. Ephesians 3:20: "Now to him who is able to do far more abundantly than all that we ask or think, according to the power at work within us, to him be glory in the church and in Christ Jesus throughout all generations, forever and ever. Amen."

## Chapter 2

5. Ron French, "World War II Created Health Insurance Perk," Detroit News, September 26, 2006. Online link has expired, but a summary is available at https://www.cheersandgears.com/forums/topic/12195-world-war-ii-created-health-insurance-perk/.

6. Original source no longer available. Year confirmed by Stephanie Smith, Executive Assistant at Everence (formerly Mennonite Mutual Aid Association).

## Chapter 3

7.  Jacob S. Hacker, The Road to Nowhere: The Genesis of President Clinton's Plan for Health Security (Princeton, NJ: Princeton University Press, 1999), chapter 1 at http://www.nytimes.com/books/first/h/hacker-nowhere.html.

8.  "Barberton Rescue Mission, Inc., d/b/a The Christian Brotherhood Newsletter, Appellee, v. The Insurance Division of the Iowa Department of Commerce," Appellant, November 25, 1998, https://law.justia.com/cases/iowa/supreme-court/1998/96-2280-2281.html.

## Chapter 6

9.  As of August 2019.

10. Merriam-Webster's Collegiate Dictionary, 11th Edition (Springfield, MA, 2004), 689.

## Chapter 7

11. "Safe-harbor" states are Alabama, Alaska, Arizona, Arkansas, Florida, Georgia, Idaho, Illinois, Indiana, Iowa, Kansas, Kentucky, Louisiana, Maine, Maryland, Michigan, Mississippi, Missouri, Nebraska, New Hampshire, North Carolina, Oklahoma, Pennsylvania, South Dakota, Texas, Utah, Virginia, Washington, Wisconsin, and Wyoming.

12. As of 2019, the Samaritan Board includes nine members—six elected by members, as well as Founder and President Ted Pittenger and two of his appointees.

## Chapter 8

13. Will Dunham, "Timeline: Milestones in Obama's quest for healthcare reform," Reuters, March 21, 2010, https://www.reuters.com/article/us-usa-healthcare-timeline/

timeline-milestones-in-obamas-quest-for-healthcare-reform-idUSTRE62L0JA20100322.

14. From an unpublished letter from Tom Perriello to Nancy Pelosi and Steny Hoyer, Washington, DC, October 15, 2009.

15. Ray King, "God amazes us again," Samaritan Ministries Christian Health Care Newsletter, June 2011, 1.

16. Ibid.

## Chapter 10

17. "Samaritan Ministries Guidelines for Health Care Sharing," November 2013, 19.

18. Ibid., 18.

19. This happened during three consecutive months in late 2014 and early 2015.

## Chapter 12

20. Sadly, stuffing day went by the wayside as membership grew. Collating and stuffing upwards of 50,000 newsletters became impractical.

21. The exception to that rule is T-Shirt Tuesday. Samaritan employees are allowed to wear T-shirts or sweatshirts on the first Tuesday of each month (with proper modesty). That tradition started one Tuesday in 2013 when Ted forgot to change out of a T-shirt before coming into work one Tuesday, thus violating his own rule. He did the only sensible thing: Declared the first Tuesday of each month T-Shirt Tuesday.

## Chapter 14

22. You can find the full list of states with safe-harbor laws in the notes for chapter 7.

# APPENDIX 1

## Samaritan Ministries International's Foundational Principles

We believe the following Biblical principles are basic to the life of every believer; therefore they are foundational to our health care sharing ministry:

**Jesus Christ is our Provider for every need.** As the Creator of all things, He is the only One with all the resources necessary to meet every need that occurs in His creation.

**Our needs are more than physical.** Human beings are more than just a collection of cells, and we have needs that go beyond the physical body. Our members come together to meet the financial, physical, and spiritual aspects of each medical need.

**God has made us stewards of His resources.** As a first line of defense, members of the Body of Christ are responsible to use the resources they've been given by God to care for themselves, their family, and others.

**Our local Christian church offers us support.** We seek to support and supplement the local Body, not replace it. We depend on local Christian church leaders to provide accountability for the Samaritan members under their care.

**Mankind is the crown of His Creation.** Because we bear the image of God, we are to respect all human life at all stages of development. Therefore, we live according to Biblical principles in all aspects of our lives by treating our bodies as temples of the Holy Spirit.

# APPENDIX 2

## Samaritan Ministries International's Member Statement of Faith

- I believe in the triune God of the Bible. He is one God who is revealed in three distinct Persons—God the Father, God the Son, and God the Holy Spirit. Genesis 1:26; Luke 1:35, 3:21-22; 2 Corinthians 13:14; Matthew 28:18-20

- I believe Jesus Christ was God in the flesh, and continues to be such even after His resurrection—fully God and fully man. He was born of a virgin, lived a sinless life, died on the cross to pay the penalty for our sins, was bodily resurrected on the third day, and now is seated in the Heavens at the right hand of God the Father. Isaiah 7:14, 9:6; Matthew 1:22-23, 26:64; Mark 16:19; Luke 24:38-40; John 1:1-2, 1:14, 1:29, 2:18-21, 5:18, 8:46; Acts 2:32-33; 1 Corinthians 15:3-4, 15:20-21; 2 Corinthians 5:21; Colossians 1:15-20, 2:9; Hebrews 1:1-4, 4:14-15, 7:26, 9:11-14, 10:10-12; 1 Peter 2:22-24; 1 John 3:5

- I believe that all people have sinned and fallen short of God's glory and can be saved from eternal death only through faith in Jesus Christ, whose atoning death and resurrection secures for us eternal life. Jeremiah 17:9; John 3:3, 14:6, 20:30-31; Romans 3:9-11, 3:23, 5:12-21, 10:8-13; Ephesians 2:8-9

# GLOSSARY

**Affordable Care Act:** The health care law signed in 2011 that required most US citizens to have health insurance. Members of health care sharing ministries were given an exemption from that mandate.

**Alliance of Health Care Sharing Ministries:** A 501 (s)(6) trade organization representing the interests of health care sharing ministries to government.

**Christian Health Care Newsletter:** The formal name of the Samaritan Ministries newsletter and a division of Samaritan Ministries International.

**Christian Healthcare Ministries:** A health care sharing ministry based in Ohio, formerly known as Christian Brotherhood Newsletter.

**Groundhog:** The Samaritan Ministries database, so called because the original launch target date was February 2.

**Guidelines:** Samaritan Ministries' document that defines membership requirements and sharing rules.

**Health care sharing ministry (HCSM):** A noninsurance approach to health care that enables Christian families to help one another with medical expenses.

**International Cabinet (IC):** The management group that oversees Samaritan Ministries operations and carries out decisions of the Board of Directors.

**Medi-Share:** A health care sharing ministry based in Florida

**Member Services (MS):** A department in Samaritan Ministries that communicates with members about membership issues and Needs and oversees processing of Needs.

**Morning Center:** A ministry created by Samaritan Ministries to help underserved women through pregnancy and birth.

**Need:** Medical expenses related to a condition that fits within Samaritan Ministries' Guidelines for sharing among members. Capitalized in official documentation.

**Pittenger Paint & Paper:** Ted Pittenger's business before starting Samaritan Ministries.

**Prayer Guide:** Monthly publication sent with the Christian Health Care Newsletter that includes daily suggestions for prayer for members whose Needs are being shared that month.

**Prorating:** A method of avoiding a sharing backup of member Needs by matching the dollar amount of Needs in a month to the amount of Shares available. For example, if there was only enough share money in a month for 80 percent of the Needs submitted, then only 80 percent of the need amounts would be shared. A $1,000 prorated need would only have $800 shared.

**Samaritan Basic:** A membership level with a lower monthly Share and higher level of initial cost responsibility.

**Samaritan Classic:** A membership level with a higher monthly Share and a lower level of initial cost responsibility.

# GLOSSARY

**Samaritan Ministries International:** The health care sharing ministry started by Ted A. Pittenger that began sharing in October 1994.

**Samaritan Motor Vehicle:** The Samaritan Ministries sharing ministry that provided for Needs stemming from motor-vehicle-related incidents, now incorporated into both Samaritan Basic and Samaritan Classic.

**Save to Share:** The voluntary Samaritan Ministries ministry that provides for Needs over $250,000.

**Share:** The monthly amount that one Samaritan Ministries member household sends to another household. Capitalized in official documentation.

**Special Prayer Need (SPN):** A member's Need that is not shareable under the Samaritan Guidelines—e.g., a pre-existing condition or extensive dental work—but is communicated to members so they may voluntarily give extra to the member.

**Subscribers, Subscriber Services:** The original term for members of Samaritan Ministries. Since members were actually subscribing to a newsletter that directed where they could send their Share, they were known as subscribers.

# SOURCES

## Interviews, 2009-2018

Samaritan Ministries International employees and family, including Ted and Shari Pittenger, James Lansberry, Ray King, Bryan Evans, DeWayne Arington, Cameron Easley, Jason Morris, Barb Lange, Seth Ben-Ezra, Justin Easley, Colton Evans, Micah Repke, Anthony Hopp, Dwayne Carr, Steve McHugh, Michelle Arington, and Anne (King) Repke, as well as General Counsel Brian Heller.

Former Alliance of Health Care Sharing Ministries consultant Joe Guarino.

Members Tracy Kamprath, Bob and Kelly Rutan, Jay Moore, James Reid, Paul and Elizabeth Garcia, former member Ron Walker, and "Maria."

Grace-Marie Turner of the Galen Institute; John Graham, formerly of the Pacific Research Institute and now with the Department of Health and Human Services; Devon Herrick, formerly of the National Center for Policy Analysis; and Dr. Jane Orient of the Association of American Physicians and Surgeons.

Laura Goodall of First Baptist Church, Hammond, Indiana.

Mike Martin and Andy Tharp of The Karis Group.

## Print and Online

Richard Ebeling, "National Health Insurance and the Welfare State, Part 1" The Future of Freedom Foundation, January 1, 1994, www.fff.org/explore-freedom/article/national-health-insurance-welfare-state-part-1/; part 2, February 1, 1994, www.fff.org/explore-freedom/article/national-health-insurance-welfare-state-part-2/; part 3, March 1, 1994, www.fff.org/explore-freedom/article/national-health-insurance-welfare-state-part-3/.

"A Detailed Timeline of the Healthcare Debate portrayed in 'The System'" is no longer available on the PBS website, but a summary is available in Jacob S. Hacker's book, The Road to Nowhere: The Genesis of President Clinton's Plan for Health Security (Princeton, NJ: Princeton University Press, 1999), chapter 1 at http://www.nytimes.com/books/first/h/hacker-nowhere.html.

"The Health Security Act of 1993," https://www.ibiblio.org/pub/academic/political-science/Health-Security-Act/foley-mitchell-letter.txt.

Ron French, "World War II Created Health Insurance Perk," Detroit News, September 26, 2006. Online link has expired, but a summary is available at https://www.cheersandgears.com/forums/topic/12195-world-war-ii-created-health-insurance-perk/.

John K. Iglehart, "Managed Competition," New England Journal of Medicine 328 (April 22, 1993):1208-1212. www.nejm.org/doi/full/10.1056/NEJM199304223281627.

# ACKNOWLEDGMENTS

Many people, both inside Samaritan Ministries International and outside, shared the burden of creating this book.

Thanks go mainly to Ted Pittenger, Founder and President of Samaritan Ministries, and his wife, Shari, for their multiple readings of the manuscripts.

Thanks to Ray King, Special Counsel to the President at SMI, for his wisdom.

Thanks to Jed Stuber, Director of Member Communications, for his flexibility.

Thanks to James McDonald VI, Director of Marketing, for his encouragement and guidance.

Thanks to Brian Heller, General Counsel, for his precision.

Thanks to all who gave of their time for interviews.

Thanks to outside editors Ken Walker (KenWalkerWriter.com) and Erin K. Brown (WriteEditor.net).

Thanks to the team at Michael T. Hamilton's Good Comma Editing (GoodCommaEditing.com) for proofreading and to Deborah and Michael E. Hamilton's team at Hamilton Strategies, Inc., for getting the word out.

Thank you to Aloha Publishing (AlohaPublishing.com) for their help in taking us across the finish line with this book.

## SHARING THE BURDEN

Thanks also to my wife, Annette, for her encouragement every step of the way.

And thanks to our Father in Heaven, for walking with Samaritan Ministries from the first step.

Michael Miller

# ABOUT THE AUTHORS

**Michael Miller** has been able to use his talents "for The Kingdom" at Samaritan Ministries International since July 2008. At Samaritan, he contributes to the newsletter, social media, and public relations teams. He worked at the Journal Star in Peoria, Illinois, from 1978 to 2008, as a reporter, copy editor, section editor, and columnist. Mike and his wife, Annette, have four children and two cats and live in central Illinois. He is a diehard St. Louis Cardinals fan.

**Ted A. Pittenger** is the Founder and President of Samaritan Ministries International. He and his wife, Shari, and their six children followed the Lord's leading to start the ministry and have witnessed the Lord's blessing over the past 25 years. Ted and Shari have been married over 40 years, and home educated their six children through high school. It is their great joy that their children walk in the truth (3 John 4). Ted and Shari make their home in rural Washington, Illinois—just across the river from Peoria.

# CHRISTIANS HELPING CHRISTIANS WITH THEIR HEALTH CARE

When the Body of Christ comes together to pray, encourage, and provide for one another, burdens are lifted, and God is glorified. This applies to all areas of life, including health care.

Health care sharing in Samaritan Ministries is a Biblical way to help your family and care for your brothers and sisters in Christ. Every month, Samaritan members help one another with their health care needs by praying, encouraging, and giving to each other financially.

We are a community of believers in Jesus Christ who are following New Testament principles to meet one another's health care needs, as an extension of the local church.

When we trust God in everything, we trust Him for our health care.

For more information about joining Samaritan Ministries International, call 877-764-2426.